Walks from ⸱⸱⸱⸱⸱

By

Geoff Holland

First published in Great Britain in 2008 by Trailguides Limited.
Second edition published in Great Britain in 2010 by Trailguides Limited.
Third edition published in Great Britain in 2012 by Trailguides Limited.
www.trailguides.co.uk

ISBN 978-1-905444-51-9

The route diagrams in this book are based upon 1925-1940 Ordnance Survey One-Inch maps updat-
ed by field trips and site visits.

Trailguides Limited
35 Carmel Road South
Darlington
Co Durham DL3 8DQ

Cover design by Steve Gustard
Artwork by Trailguides Limited

FOREVER

Together in these hills
of cotton grass
and quiet cleughs
we walk forever
young and fancy free

Geoff Holland

CONTENTS

	Page
INTRODUCTION	
1. The Book	5
2. Wooler	7
3. Northumberland National Park	9
4. The Cheviot Hills	11
5. Access & The Right to Roam	12
6. The Walks	14
7. The Weather	16
8. The Maps	17
9. Accommodation & Facilities	18
THE WALKS	
1. Cold Law Considered	21
2. A Walk to the Pole	31
3. The Road to Tom Tallon`s Crag	39
4. The Hart Heugh Glidders	48
5. High Above the College Burn	59
6. The Eastern Fringe	69
7. From Valley Floor to Summit Cairn	79
8. The Lambden Valley Hills	88
POSTSCRIPT	**98**
APPENDIX	
Ferguson Grading System	99
The Author	102
Walking North East	103
Acknowledgements	104
Disclaimer	104

Front cover. The track to Gleadscleugh. Walk 3 The Road to Tom Tallon's Crag. Back cover. Winter on Hedgehope Hill. Walk 7 From Valley Floor to Summit Cairn.

INTRODUCTION

1. The Book

I first stumbled across `Walks from Wooler`, a book by W. Ford Robertson, at a Book Fair in Tynemouth Station a number of years ago. A quick thumb through the slightly `foxed` pages and my curiosity was aroused but, at £17.50, I hesitated. Despite what I thought was a pretty determined attempt on my part to haggle, the bookseller would not budge on the price and I walked away.

Back at home, I regretted my decision so I decided that the very next time I saw a copy of the book I would buy it. However, it was to be another three years before I came across it again and, this time around, the price was a very modest £6. Sensing a bargain, I made no attempt to barter and before you could say " all things come to those who wait", I had unlocked my wallet and "splashed the cash"! I was not disappointed.

Born on the 28th July 1867 at the Berwickshire farm of Nottylees, on the south bank of the River Tweed, W. Ford Robertson`s father died when he was only 3 years old. Despite this sad and premature loss, William went on to study medicine at Edinburgh University and, on graduation in 1891, he took up his first professional position as a house physician at the Edinburgh Royal Infirmary.

Displaying a talent as a medical scientist, much of the remainder of William`s illustrious career was dedicated to research into the treatment of mental diseases. He died in 1923, at the age of 56 years, and his services to science were recognised by the award, to his widow, of a Civil List pension of £100.

Before his death, W. Ford Robertson had purchased an old property near Wooler and had turned it into "a charming holiday retreat with a most beautiful garden, in which he could carry out experiments in hybridising flowers, and from where he could sally forth to explore the surrounding countryside".

The book, `Walks from Wooler` was a direct result of the time he spent exploring the area and it was to be his final work. It was published 3 years after his death because, as the Reverend W.I. Moran said in the foreward to the book, "......so many of us felt that the rich fruits of such labours ought not to be lost and that to lovers of the district it supplies a very real need".

It is now more than 80 years since W. Ford Robertson wandered the hills and valleys surrounding the north Northumberland town of Wooler. Since then, the motor car has made access to the countryside so much easier and, with ever more leisure time to play with, a greater number of people are now heading for the hills. However, the Cheviot Hills remain remarkably quiet and it is not unusual to walk all day without meeting another person. In this respect, very little seems to have changed since 1926.

But change is inevitable, however slowly it may creep upon us. It reaches all corners of the globe, even the sleepy heights and hollows of England's most northerly hills, and as I read and re-read 'Walks from Wooler', I began to wonder what affect, if any, had these changes had on the route descriptions set out in this wonderful little book. Could these routes still be followed with relative ease and was the book, after all the intervening years, still relevant? I just had to find out.

To satisfy my curiosity, I selected a 9 mile, "half-day walk" which I knew followed easy and relatively familiar territory. This would, I thought, be the 'acid test'. So, armed with my slightly dog-eared copy of his 'Walks from Wooler', I

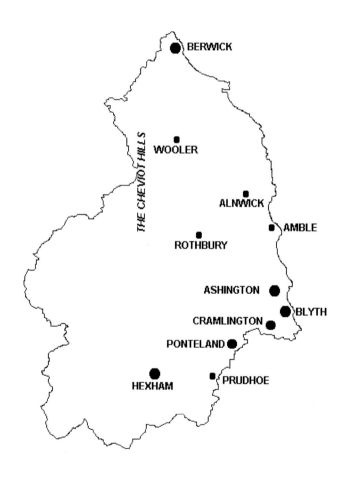

was ready, on a clear, crisp morning in October 2006, to follow in the footsteps of W. Ford Robertson. The results of this pleasant stroll into the past were published a year later in the 20ᵗʰ Birthday Issue of `The Northumbrian`, a bi-monthly magazine for people who love `England`s finest county`. And that, I thought, would be that.

But curiosity is a funny old thing. It takes hold and is very difficult to shake off. It niggles away and there seems to be no instant or easy cure. I kept thinking about the other walks in the book, after all there were 185 pages bulging with 59 more walking routes and a huge amount of fascinating information. I kept thinking about " the 9.25 a.m. train from Wooler, going north " and what it must have been like to alight at Kirknewton Station, in the shadow of Yeavering Bell, at the start of a "whole-day walk".

Was it just nostalgia tugging at my sleeve or was my journey into a walking past not yet complete. I was soon to realise that, in reality, the journey was just beginning.

A final glance back at Hedgehope Hill.
Walk 7 From Valley Floor to Summit Cairn.

2. Wooler

The small, stone-built town of Wooler, perched high above Wooler Water, is a natural gateway to the Cheviot Hills and to a `big slice` of the Northumberland National Park.

The area, as a whole, is covered with the footprints of ancient history and the bloodline of Wooler is believed to date back to pre-Bronze Age settlements. In 1107 it was little more than a hamlet, described as being "situated in an ill-cultivated country under the influence of vast mountains, from whence it is subject to impetuous rains".

In 1199 a licence was granted to hold a market every Thursday and the town soon became the social, political and economic centre of the Glendale area. Fuelled during medieval times by a strong woollen industry, Wooler became one of the four wealthiest towns in Northumberland.

Over the years the town has been subjected to a variety of attacks, with the Scottish raids of 1340 and 1409 being particularly destructive. In 1402 the nearby Battle of Homildon Hill resulted in the Scottish forces, led by Archibald, Earl of Douglas, being soundly defeated by the forces of the Earl of Northumberland and his son Harry Hotspur. News of the battle is immortalised in Shakespeare's play, 'Henry IV'.

The town, like many other towns and cities, suffered a number of serious fires during the 18th and 19th centuries with the fire of 1863 being particularly devastating. As a result, much of the High Street was re-built.

The routing of the Newcastle to Edinburgh road through the town in 1830 and the arrival of the railway in 1887 brought further affluence to Wooler.

There are a number of interesting buildings in the town and some of these have been given Listed status. A keen eye will spot the 17th century-built Angel Inn with its white painted façade and oriel window, the 1910-built 'Arts and Crafts' style Black Bull Hotel with an unusual black painted finish and gold motifs and the Red Lion, dating from 1671 and sporting a late 19th century bay window with a castellated parapet. There are, of course, many more and an exploration of the various 'nooks and crannies' will be well rewarded.

The renowned 19th century social reformer Josephine Butler was born near Wooler in 1828. She played a major role in improving conditions for women in both education and public health and her most famous publication was the 1896 'Personal Reminiscences of a Great Crusade'. She died in 1906 and is buried in St. Gregory's Church, Kirknewton.

These days, Wooler is a popular destination for walkers, cyclists and day visitors and offers a wide range of facilities, details of which are set out on pages 18 -20.

The Arts and Crafts style Black Bull.

3. Northumberland National Park

In 1926, the same year as `Walks from Wooler` rolled off the printing press, the historian George Macaulay Trevelyan wrote, in his essay entitled `The Middle Marches`, " In Northumberland alone, both heaven and earth are seen; we walk all day on long ridges, high enough to give far views of moor and valley, and a sense of solitude above the world below" adding "It is a land of far horizons".

Although written long before the National Parks and Access to the Countryside Act 1949 made provision for the designation of National Parks, these words perfectly express why the hill country of Northumberland should be given special recognition.

The Northumberland National Park, which covers an area of 1049 square kilometres (405 square miles), was, on the 6th April 1956, the ninth National Park to be officially designated. It is the least populated of all of the fifteen current National Parks with an estimated population of two people per square kilometre. The symbol of the National Park is the curlew.

There are three main land uses; farming, woodland and forestry and military. The National Park contains a huge number of Sites of Special Scientific Interest,

Special Areas of Conservation, National Nature Reserves, Listed Buildings, Scheduled Ancient Monuments and, of course, a proportion of Hadrian`s Wall World Heritage Site. The highest point is the peat covered, 815 metre (2676 feet) high summit of The Cheviot.

The College Valley looking north.
Walk 5 High Above the College Burn.

There are currently three Northumberland National Park Information Centres, all of which can offer the visitor a wide range of information and advice, and these are located at Rothbury (Rothbury National Park Centre is Church House, Church Street, Rothbury, NE65 7UP, telephone number **01669620887**), Ingram (Ingram Visitor Centre, Powburn, Alnwick, NE66 4LT, telephone number **01665578890)** and Once Brewed (Once Brewed National Park Centre, Military Road, Bardon Mill, Hexham, NE47 7AN, telephone number **01434344396).**

As a consequence of drastic cuts in public expenditure post-2010 the centres at both Rothbury and Ingram are currently under review. Alternative ways of maintaining an information presence in these locations are being actively pursued. So for those walkers wishing to visit these centres it would be advisable to first visit **www.northumberlandnationalpark.org.uk** to find out about the current status of the centres and, if they are still in operation, their opening times.

The Cheviot from Long Crags.
Walk 7 From Valley Floor to Summit Cairn.

4. The Cheviot Hills

The Cheviot Hills are England's most northerly hills and cover an area of some 1035 square kilometres (400 square miles). They rise and fall along the northern edge of England, rolling down into Scotland in small, green, rounded waves. In the great scheme of matters mountainous, they are not especially big hills with the highest, The Cheviot, standing at a height of 815 metres (2674 feet). But with distant views to endless horizons and clouds billowing overhead, you cannot help but feel that this is truly big country.

The Cheviot Hills are volcanic in origin with deep, narrow valleys radiating from the central core. They are of national nature conservation importance, supporting extensive areas of blanket bog and heather moorland. They are remote and sparsely populated with vehicular access being restricted to the valley floors.

In the opinion of W. Ford Robertson, "The main features of the Cheviot Hills that make them a paradise for the pedestrian are their peaceful, lonely glens, their wide expanses of bracken-clad hillside….and their broad heathery moors". Exactly!

This is, indeed, ideal walking territory where hours, even days, can pass without a chance meeting with another lonely wandering soul. In these wild, expansive hills the DNA of a long and fascinating past lies beneath every single footstep you take. As the wind sweeps across the seemingly endless curve of hills and through deep and remote valleys you will feel an unrivalled sense of isolation. Here the curlew is king and solitude is his queen.

11

The track across the heather moor to Tom Tallon's Crag.
Walk 3 The Road to Tom Tallon's Crag.

5. Access & The Right to Roam

When W. Ford Robertson sallied forth across the Cheviot Hills in the early part of the 20th century, the mass trespass on Kinder Scout in the Peak District was still a `public awareness campaign` waiting to happen. However, the debate regarding the `freedom to roam` had already begun and, by the time his book was published in 1926, a `freedom to roam` bill had been introduced into Parliament each year between 1884 and 1914 and had, on every occasion, been duly defeated.

Mindful, therefore, of the potential for conflict between landowners and walkers, W. Ford Robertson included a short section in his book entitled, "Note on the Law of Trespass". He pointed out that, in respect of the area covered by the walks, "there has always been a generous latitude shown by proprietors and tenants with regard to trespass upon unenclosed land" adding that "if you conduct yourself as ladies and gentlemen should…..you are welcomed, and not regarded as a nuisance".

And that is how it remained for nigh on 80 years, with regular walkers ignoring the definitive map and making their own tracks across these wide open spaces. However, for the occasional visitor, ignorant of common practice, the position was totally unsatisfactory.

Whilst there was a generous number of public footpaths and bridleways throughout the Cheviot Hills, together with a handful of `permitted footpaths` negotiated with landowners, very few of the hills enjoyed public rights of way to their actual tops. Of the six summits in the Cheviot Hills exceeding 2000 feet in height, only two, The Cheviot and Windy Gyle, were served by public rights of way and then only as a direct consequence of the Pennine Way crossing their respective summits.

Looking back up the Harthope Valley.
Walk 7 From Valley Floor to Summit Cairn.

Thankfully, this unsatisfactory and often confusing situation, was consigned to history on the 28th May 2005 when the Countryside and Rights of Way Act 2000 finally became law. This landmark piece of legislation allowed walkers and runners to roam freely on designated 'access land' with no need to keep to official footpaths or bridleways.

The Act did, however, give landowners and farmers permission to restrict the 'right to roam' for up to 28 days each year. Also, some areas of the Cheviot Hills are managed grouse moors so it is important to be aware of the restrictions that may apply to walking with dogs. To find out more about out the 'right to roam' and whether any general or specific restrictions apply to an area of the Cheviot Hills you intend to explore in the near future a visit to the website **www.naturalengland.org.uk** will give you all the necessary information.

The new 'access land' is now shown on the latest editions of the Ordnance Survey Explorer map (OL 16) marked with a light yellow coloured background and, at many entry points to the 'access land', stiles and gates carry the new 'access land' waymarking symbol (a brown 'stick' man in a brown circle).

6. The Walks

The title spells it out, loud and clear. Every walk in W. Ford Robertson`s book starts from Wooler, either by taking one of the roads leading out of the town, such as Cheviot Street or Ramsey`s Lane, or by wandering down to the station and catching "the morning or afternoon train to Kirknewton" or "the forenoon train to Hedgeley". All very straightforward.

The 1926 walks are divided into three categories; "short walks", "half-day walks" and "whole-day walks" and, in many cases, the first few miles of a walk are the same as two or three other walks in the book. After all, the routes into the hills from Wooler are not infinite.

As we know, modes of transport have changed hugely since 1926. The passenger train to Kirknewton and Hedgeley stopped `puffing` out of Wooler in 1930 and the motor car has now made access to the hills considerably easier. It is now possible to start walks from a greater variety of locations.

The walks in this book, therefore, do not follow W. Ford Robertson`s footprints step for step. I have used the 1926 book more as an inspiration to get out into the hills to compare the rambling world of a more innocent age with my own present day walking world. Only two of my walks start from Wooler, although all of the walks are centred on the town, with a visit before or after the outing always an easy option.

There are fewer walks in this book than in the 1926 book but the variety of places visited is not compromised. The vast majority of the ground covered by these walks will have had W. Ford Robertson`s well-worn `tackety boots` firmly planted on them at some time or other.

The walks in this book should be well within the capabilities of any reasonably fit walker, sensibly `kitted out` for potentially changeable mountain weather. They also make excellent training circuits for those who prefer to run on the fells.

The clothing available to the 1920`s walker was basic, to say the least, by today`s hi-tech standards. There were no shock-absorbing, high-grade aluminium walking poles to ease the strain, no computer-compatible GPS units to aid navigation, no super-light, waterproof and breathable outer shells to shed the rain and no zip-out micro fleeces to keep in the warmth.

"Equipment is", W. Ford Robertson wrote, "of the utmost importance". He felt that "Tackety boots (not too heavy), or rubber soles, and a stout stick" were an essential part of a ramblers wardrobe. He thought that "a light waterproof should be carried" if only to, "put between yourself and the grass when you rest". He listed a variety of items he considered "important in an emergency" including,

The former Kirknewton Station.
Walk 5 High Above the College Burn.

"a compass, a sharp penknife, two yards of strong twine, a box of matches, a drinking cup, a clean folded handkerchief and a few ounces of whiskey, brandy or aromatic spirit of ammonia".

In a chapter entitled "Rules for the Rambler" he offered further "Hints to the Pedestrian" and you will stumble upon many of those hints as you read through the eight walks in this book.

The route descriptions set out in this book are easy to follow and contain Grid References at key points. They should be used in conjunction with either of the two recommended maps. The walks have all been graded in accordance with the Ferguson Grading System (`FGS`) and the actual grading is set out at the end of each individual walk. A detailed explanation of the FGS and how individual gradings are determined is set out on pages 99-101 of the Appendix to this book.

A day wandering in the hills offers an ideal means of escape from an increasingly regulated way of life. Experienced walkers and runners are usually sensible sort of folk with a desire to leave only footprints. They know, for instance, to leave gates and property as they find them, to protect plants and animals, to take their litter home and to avoid starting fires. This is all pretty basic stuff. However, if you want to read more about the Countryside and Moorland Codes, before you tackle any of the walks in this book, just log onto **www.naturalengland.org.uk**. It is all there in black and white.

Needless to say, W. Ford Robertson, as thorough as ever, had ideas on how walkers should conduct themselves when out and about in the countryside. He pointed out that, "A committee of experienced Cheviot Hill trampers have gradually formulated nine `Rules for the Hills`, the adoption of which I would strongly recommend to every pedestrian who roams these wilds". A close examination of these rules reveals a distinct similarity to the Countryside Code, although the one which requires the walker to, "Stop now and again to admire the view" appears to have been mislaid somewhere along the way. Nevertheless, sound advice!

The Lambden Valley and the distant Schil.
Walk 8 The Lambden Valley Hills.

7. The Weather

The prevailing south westerly wind rushes in from the distant Atlantic Ocean shedding the majority of its precipitation before reaching the Cheviot Hills. The average annual rainfall on the high ground is 110 cm., less than half the rainfall of more popular mountain playgrounds such as the Lake District and the Scottish Highlands.

The driest months of the year tend to be March, April and June whilst the wettest are November, December and January. The latter part of August, the peak of the holiday season, is also often unsettled. During January, February and March cold north winds can make walking on the high tops particularly demanding although huge snowfalls are rare.

This said, walking in the Cheviot Hills can, at any time of the year, produce surprises. A cold, clear February day, an early morning frost and a bright blue, uncluttered sky can leave you with memories that will long outlive a day spent tramping the hills at the height of an English summer. If you are a regular walker in the Cheviot Hills it is unlikely that you will, in the fullness of time, escape the full spectrum of local weather. It is even possible that it will all arrive during a single walk.

Langlee and Housey Crags from The Cheviot.
Walk 2 A Walk to the Pole.

8. The Maps

A map of the area, based on the Ordnance Survey Map, was supplied with the 1926 book. Measuring approximately 13½ inches by 15½ inches and on a scale of 4¼ inches to 5 miles, the black and white map is a jumble of solid and broken lines. The solid lines represent rivers, burns, roads etc whilst the broken lines, which are all numbered, indicate the routes of the various walks in the book. The tops of the hills are marked by a triangle with the height printed alongside. To be honest, the map is not something you would wish to rely on when out and about on a perfect summer's day, let alone in a force 8 gale with rain driving incessantly into your face but, to a generation who did not have ready access to more sophisticated maps, they were undoubtedly useful.

Today two maps cover the Cheviot Hills: the Ordnance Survey Explorer (1: 25000) OL 16 and the Harvey Superwalker (1: 40000) The Cheviot Hills. Which one you choose is down to personal taste.

Looking down to the Carey Burn.
Walk 4 The Hart Heugh Glidders.

9. Accommodation & Facilities

There are more than sufficient hotels, guest houses, self catering accommodation and caravan & camping sites within shouting distance of the centre of Wooler to suit most tastes and budgets. It is not for me to make any specific recommendations, I will leave that up to the experts.

So, for all your accommodation requirements just talk to the Wooler Tourist Information Centre at Cheviot Centre, 12 Padgepool Place, Wooler, Northumberland NE71 6BL, telephone number **01668282123**. Alternatively, contact any of the Northumberland National Park Information Centres mentioned in Section 3 of this Introduction on page 9.

There are a fair few shops, cafes and other facilities in and around the centre of Wooler, so most visitors to the town ought to be adequately catered for. There are shops selling books both new & secondhand, gifts, flowers, newspapers & magazines, groceries and clothing. There is a dispensing chemist, a garden centre, cycle hire, a butcher, a garage, a pottery and much more besides. For further information log onto the Wooler Community website, **www.wooler.org.uk**.

In a book of walks centred around Wooler it would be unforgivable not to in-

A long way from the sea.

clude a few paragraphs about one of the town's best loved institutions and main accommodation providers, the Wooler Youth Hostel.

The Youth Hostel Association of Great Britain sprang into life in 1930 in order to meet a rapidly growing demand for simple accommodation for walkers and cyclists. Within months, the organisation had changed its name to the YHA (England and Wales) and at the same time, independent associations were formed for both Scotland and Ireland. Growth was rapid and before long a large number of hostels had opened up with the first formal Northumberland hostel opening at Wallington in May 1931.

In 1932, the first Wooler Youth Hostel was opened by Sir Charles Trevelyan, the Third Baronet of Wallington, a keen supporter of the Youth Hostel movement and brother of the historian George Macaulay Trevelyan. The hostel was housed in the town's old railway station with the waiting rooms being converted into accommodation for men, on one side of the tracks, and for women on the other side. A sense of decency was, therefore, preserved! Whilst passenger trains had stopped running to and from the station two years earlier, a goods service was still operational.

On the evening of the 3rd September 1939, just over 24 hours after the declaration of World War II, hostellers helped to fit blackout curtains to the windows of the hostel and the buildings, which had been leased from LNER, were returned to the owners. They were never again used as a hostel.

The town was without a hostel until October 1953 when the current building, which had been built in the early 1940's as a Women's Land Army hostel, was purchased by the YHA for the sum of £1,000. The building, which had been converted by a team of volunteers, opened its doors to visitors in August 1954 and the first wardens of this new hostel came from the Fenwick Youth Hostel which had closed in May 1954.

The building underwent substantial renovation in 1991, including the installation of a much appreciated central heating system. Further improvements followed. However, a black cloud loomed on the horizon and, in 2006, Wooler Youth Hostel was named as one of 32 hostels in the national network earmarked for closure.

Wooler Youth Hostel.

However, a 'White Knight' arrived in the form of the Glendale Trust and, with the support of the Northern Rock Foundation, managed to raise the sum of £250,000 to purchase the hostel and a further £60,000 to upgrade it to a 'three star visit Britain rating'.

The day was saved and the hostel is now run by the Trust, under an arrangement with the YHA, on a highly successful basis. Further improvements continue to be carried out and expectations for future growth in visitor numbers are high.

The hostel is located at 30 Cheviot Street and bookings can be made online at **www.yha.org.uk** or by telephoning **01668281365**.

The valley of the Carey Burn.
Walk 1 Cold Law Considered.

WALK 1: COLD LAW CONSIDERED

"The Backwood Burn is one of the most pleasant places within easy reach of Wooler", wrote W. Ford Robertson, adding that "nature has most cunningly hidden it away in the heart of the hills". It tumbles down the south-eastern flanks of Cold Law and joins the Harthope Burn one mile short of the Carey Burn Bridge. On this walk, as you wander across the slopes of the 452 metre high Cold Law, you will hear the chatter of nearby burns, feel the wind sweep across the neighbouring hills and enjoy lonely, faraway views.

DISTANCE: 6.25 miles (10.1 km)
ASCENT: 1214 feet (370 metres)
TERRAIN: Relatively clear paths and tracks, many green, and a stretch of tarmac
TIME: 3.5 hours
START: Carey Burn Bridge, Harthope Valley (GR NT976250)

Grid References

Carey Burn Bridge	976 250
Cattle grid	966 236
Back Wood	960 235
Carling Crags	955 244
Broadstruther	941 248
Fingerpost	948 250
Gate	965 248
Carey Burn Bridge	976 250

FGS Grading

Grading is Grading is F8 [D1, N2, T1, R2, H2]

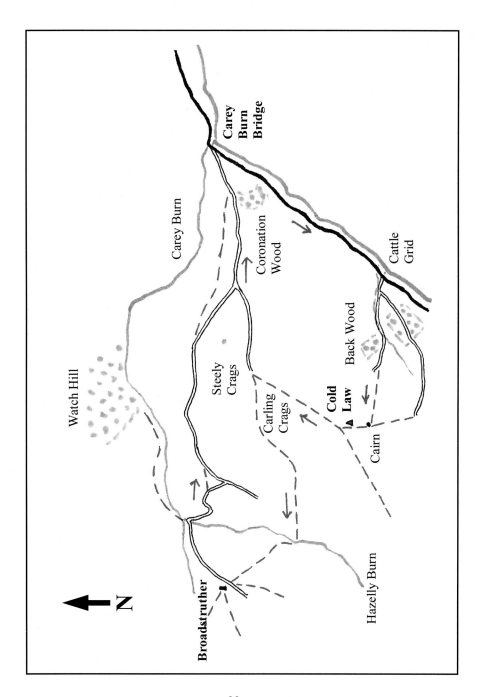

THE WALK

1. The Harthope Valley lies 5 miles south-west of Wooler and separates the two highest of the Cheviot Hills, Hedgehope Hill and the mighty Cheviot. It is a firm favourite with walkers, birdwatchers and weekend picnickers. Soon after dropping dramatically into the valley, there is limited space for parking, on the right hand side of the narrow road, on the grass immediately prior to the bridge over the Carey Burn (**GR NT976250**). Once your bootlaces are tied, your route follows the road into the valley, with the directions of W. Ford Robertson indicating that you should, "cross the Carey Burn either by the new traffic bridge, or by the footbridge". The present bridge was built in 1956 and replaced the previous one which, along with the adjacent footbridge, was washed away in the floods of 1948. Parts of the old bridge can still be seen over the right hand side balustrade. This is a pleasant and easy start to your walk, with the Harthope Burn twinkling to your left and the steep-sided Brands Hill rising darkly behind. To your right, Snear Hill climbs sharply towards the upper slopes of Cold Law.

View from the Carey Burn Bridge.

This part of the valley is popular with pheasants and, if lady luck is smiling, you might just catch a glimpse of a grey heron in full flight. After one mile of walking, as you enter a more wooded part of the valley, the Backwood Burn sneaks under the road and, almost immediately after you have crossed a cattle grid, a track climbs away from the small grassed area to your right (**GR NT966236**). This area is part of a stretch of land known as Plea Haugh, unnamed on the cur-

High above the Backwood Burn.

rent Ordnance Survey 1:25000 scale map, but mentioned by W. Ford Robertson in his 1926-published book.

2. The rough bulldozed track, which quickly splits in two, is a more `modern` intrusion on the landscape and the area around the burn would undoubtedly have been a prettier place for the lack of it back in 1926. " You will observe that this small burn tries to elude you among some tall trees", commented W. Ford Robertson, insisting that you "do not allow it to do so". He suggested that, "you may walk along the southern edge of the dene and gaze into its wooded depths (being careful not to fall in)". You must now follow the green, right hand spur of the track as it rises above the burn , with the tree-covered slopes falling away sharply to your right. Before long you will reach a small step stile standing next to a five bar gate. Climb over and cut across Pinkie Sike and then, within a handful of metres, re-cross the sike. For a short distance you will travel on a fairly damp, rising track and, after particularly wet weather, you may feel that you are actually walking along the bed of a stream. Do not despair, this swiftly becomes a pleasant grass track climbing onto open hillside, heading towards a second five bar gate. You are now leaving Back Wood (**GR NT960235**) behind and the views towards Langlee Crags, Housey Crags and Hedgehope Hill have opened up. On visiting this area, W. Ford Robertson found that Back Wood "was almost entirely composed of ancient alders" suggesting that, "it is probably no exaggeration to say that some of the trees in this wood were growing at the time of the Battle of Flodden". As the Battle of Flodden was fought in 1513 and the alder tree has a lifespan in the region of 150 years a large portion of poetic licence appears to have been liberally applied. No matter.

3. Cross over the step stile next to the gate and, after passing through a dilapidated dry stone wall, be sure to keep with the track as it turns to your right to climb directly up the steep hillside. When the gradient eases momentarily leave the track diagonally to your left on a rapidly disappearing thin trace. Aim for the tiny crag ahead and soon the walkers cairn, which lies to the south of the summit of Cold Law, comes into view. On reaching the cairn you will be given a grandstand seat. Looking southwards across the Harthope Valley, to the right of the hillside-splitting Easter Dean the jagged Langlee Crags point skywards whilst, to the south-west, the dark hills roll towards the mighty Cheviot.

The summit of Cold Law.

Now follow the single-file path to the triangulation pillar which marks the summit of this 452 metre high hill. When W. Ford Robertson stood here, soaking up the silence, this concrete pillar was just a twinkle in the eye of the Director General of the Ordnance Survey. The huge task of re-triangulating Great Britain did not begin until 1935 and was not completed until 1962. Continue to the corner of a post and wire fence, adjacent to some minor crags, and follow the fence as it tumbles downhill. At the first five bar gate, go through and, with the fence now on your right, continue straight ahead passing along the way, to your left, Carling Crags (**GR NT955244**). Before long you will arrive at another gate through the fence with an adjoining step stile. The track on the other side of the fence heads back to the Carey Burn Bridge, down the slopes of Snear Hill, a spur of Cold Law. When walking this way, W. Ford Robertson continued to follow the fence to "the junction of the Broadstruthers and Common Burns". Your route, however, turns left along a good, grass track referred to in the 1926 version of `Walks from Wooler` as "the high path from the foot of the Carey Burn to Broadstruther".

4. You are now walking in a generally westwards direction along a public foot-path which crosses a vast area of 2005-designated `access land`. The views stretch far into the distance with Watch Hill and Fredden Hill to your right and Newton Tors ahead. Soon you will pass Steely Crags downhill to your right. There are no particular route finding problems as you begin your gradual descent towards the Hazelly Burn and beyond to Broadstruther. The view is tantalising with the high tops of Hedgehope Hill, Comb Fell, The Cheviot, Broadhope Hill and Preston Hill towering above you. Standing here, seemingly miles from anywhere, you will know that once you have completed the eight walks in this book you will have visited the summits of all of these impressive looking hills. On reaching the junction with a gravel track, turn left and then, when you are 50 metres short of a track-side stone sheep stell, turn right and head downhill on a faint path passing a directional fingerpost along the way. Step over the Hazelly Burn and follow the grass track, which quickly diminishes to a thin path, to the former shepherd`s house of Broadstruther **(GR NT941248)**. Recently renovated to provide shelter for shooting parties, and standing in front of a small copse of mature trees, this single storey building, with its striking red doors and fine detail, looks pretty as a picture in this remote setting.

Pretty as a picture Broadstruther.

For the more faint-hearted.

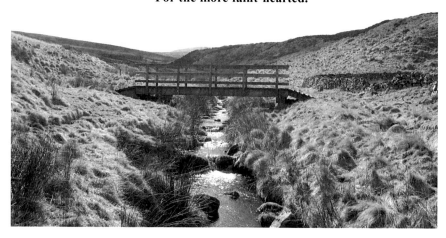

A spider's web of public footpaths and bridleways surround Broadstruther, but your onward route is quite simple. With your back to the front of the building, turn left and continue with the gravel track as it heads initially north-eastwards before curving towards the lower reaches of the Hazelly Burn. Cross the burn via a ford, or for the more faint-hearted the nearby wooden footbridge, and keep with the track as it starts to climb up the north-west facing side of Cold Law. On reaching a directional fingerpost on your left **(GR NT948250)**, leave the track and continue on a pleasant grass path for a short distance. You will then re-join the track.

Watch Hill.

5. This is the "low path" from Broadstruthers to the foot of the Carey Burn and the one which, in the opinion of W. Ford Robertson, "affords a better view of the Carey Burn valley". But first, your views are of the Broadstruther Burn as it gently meanders below you towards a meeting with the Common Burn. The striking profile of Watch Hill, with a band of trees around its lower slopes, is prominent. Follow the track as it begins to bend towards the south-east and, to your left, you will see the rock-riddled slopes of the crag-crowned Hart Heugh dropping precipitously down to the Carey Burn.

A better view of the Carey Burn valley.

Soon you will pass, uphill to your right, the remnants of a plantation of Scots Pine where there was "once a shepherd`s cottage" and somewhere, W. Ford Robertson thought was, "truly a lonely place for a human habitation". All references to this cottage have long since been wiped off the map. Keep with the track and, on reaching a five bar gate **(GR NT965248)**, go through. You have now joined the "high path", heading downhill towards the Harthope Valley and passing, as you near your journey`s end, Coronation Wood to your right. As soon as your feet touch the tarmac of the valley road, turn left, re-cross the Carey Burn Bridge and, in the wink of an eye, you will be easing off your 21st century Vibram-soled, Gortex-lined boots.

Truly a lonely place for a human habitation.

FGS Grading

Grading is F8 [D1, N2, T1, R2, H2]

Distance	1	6 – 12 miles
Navigation	2	Competent navigation skills needed
Terrain	1	50 – 75% on graded track or path 25 – 50% off track
Remoteness	2	Countryside not in close proximity to habitation – less than 20% of the route within 2 miles
Height	2	Over 125 ft per mile

The summit of The Cheviot.
Walk 2 A Walk to the Pole.

WALK 2: A WALK TO THE POLE

It is big and brawny and lies at the heart of the hills that bear the same family name. It stands between the Harthope, College and Lambden Valleys and rises to a height of 815 metres. "The flat top cannot be adequately described", commented W. Ford Robertson. He advised readers that, "it requires to be seen" and that, it seems, is exactly what subsequent generations of walkers have done. They have climbed to the roof of Northumberland. This walk follows a quiet course to the summit of the mighty Cheviot crossing, along the way, the cairn-capped top of the rarely visited Blackseat Hill.

DISTANCE: 8.5 miles (13.7 km)
ASCENT: 2380 feet (725 metres)
TERRAIN: Mixed fell with a variety of paths and tracks, some rough and boggy
TIME: 4.5 hours
START: Hawsen Burn, Harthope Valley (GR NT954225)

Grid References

Hawsen Burn	954 225
Blackseat Hill	941 226
Fence corner	915 228
Stile	914 206
Fence corner	933 221
Hawsen Burn	954 225

FGS Grading

Grading is F10 [D1, N2, T2, R2, H3]

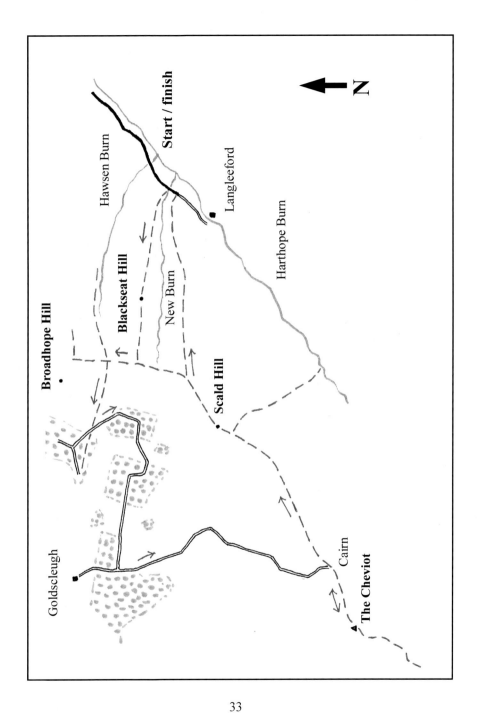

N

Broadhope Hill

Goldscleugh

Hawsen Burn

Blackseat Hill

New Burn

Start / finish

Langleeford

Harthope Burn

Scald Hill

Cairn

The Cheviot

THE WALK

1. The single track road through the Harthope Valley sets the pulses racing. The conical shaped Hedgehope Hill, the second highest in the range, dominates the view as you head towards the start of your walk. "For all walks to the top of Cheviot" wrote W. Ford Robertson, "it is of the utmost importance to make an early start" and he recommended that, "You should not be later than nine o'clock in setting out". Sound advice if you intended, like his readers back in the 1920`s, starting your walk from the stone-built streets of Wooler. But your route begins closer to the day`s main objective.

The Harthope Valley.

So, park your car on the area of grass just prior to the point where the tiny Hawsen Burn joins the Harthope Burn **(GR NT954225)** and enjoy the fine view as you pull on your revolutionary high performance four seasons walking socks. The scene is set, now let the good times roll. There is no access for cars beyond the Hawsen Burn along the road which continues towards the house of Langleeford where, W. Ford Robertson said, "the valley is beautified by fir and pine woods". Follow the road for 200 metres to the point where there is a small sign to your right indicating, `Turning Area. No Parking Please`. Leave the road and instead of following the track to the left, which is the direct and most frequently used route to the summit of The Cheviot, take the track which heads straight on through a five bar gate. You will have a small plantation and a post and wire fence to your immediate right. After a short climb and an even shorter descent the track easily fords the New Burn. As you climb away from the burn, be sure to watch out for the faint quad track which leaves the main track to your left. This is your route. Initially, this track runs alongside an exceedingly dilapidated dry stone wall before cutting across high, open moor towards the cairn-topped crag of the 461 metre high Blackseat Hill **(GR NT941226)**. The track bends behind the summit, so once parallel with the tiny walker's cairn step off the uphill treadmill for a few minutes and enjoy the airy view of the Harthope Valley and its fine collection of crags, including Housey and Langlee Crags.

Cold Law from Blackseat Hill.

2. Back on course, keep with the track as it takes a generally westwards course, with the deep valley of the New Burn prominent to your left. Meanwhile, The Cheviot makes its not insubstantial presence felt as it rises steeply behind Scald Hill. On reaching the fence, turn to your right and keep moving forwards as far

The Cheviot rises behind Scald Hill.

as a step stile, some 500 metres away. The remote Lambden Valley lies on the other side and, from this point, extends for a distance of 3½ miles before joining the broader College Valley. Cross over the step stile and continue straight ahead. To your left, The Cheviot dominates the southern side of the valley, whilst Broadhope, Preston and Coldburn Hills join forces to the north. Continue downhill on a clear path towards a forestry track and, when reached, turn left. In the years since 1926, the valley has undergone some noticeable changes. There has been much afforestation, blocks of which have been recently harvested, and the long scar of the forest road, wrapped around the head of the valley, is a less than pretty sight. Of the three properties in the valley, only Goldscleugh remains as a working farm whilst Dunsdale and Coldburn have been converted to holiday lets. The valley was much admired by W. Ford Robertson, and despite the changes and the odd blemish the valley remains a delightful place. Stay with the undulating stone track as it turns around the valley head and cuts across the lower slopes of The Cheviot. Eventually, after passing through a series of five bar gates, the track bends to the right and heads rapidly downhill to Goldscleugh. Do not follow the track downhill. Instead take the slightly rougher track to your left, keeping close to the fence as it makes a right angle turn **(GR NT915228)**. Now for the hard part of the day as you start your 1½ mile climb to the summit of the county's highest hill.

Goldscleugh from the slopes of The Cheviot.

3. Pass through the gate and, with the ragged profile of Woolhope Crag to your left, stay with the green track as it heads relentlessly upwards. You will undoubtedly wish to pause from time to time to admire the view. It should not be missed. The burn which cuts through the hillside to your immediate right is the Goldscleugh Burn which, in the words of W. Ford Robertson, "...rises near the Pole of Cheviot and enters the Lambden Burn below the cottage of the same name". Continue to follow the track and, eventually, the gradient begins to ease, as you first pass a stone shelter on the left and then a cairn on the eastern end of the summit plateau. This is "the cairn on the East Hill of Cheviot" referred to by W. Ford Robertson, with the actual summit now being, "situated less than half a mile to the south-west". Join the millstone pathway, close to a near vertical ladder stile, turn right and head the short distance to the summit triangulation pillar, perched on a substantial concrete plinth, high above a sea of peat . When W. Ford Robertson reached here, a "lightning splintered pole" marked the summit. Despite saying that, "The flat top could not be adequately described" he did indicate that it was "a vast bog, broken up by great hags, filled in wet seasons with soft black muddy peat to a depth of several feet and, at times, it is impossible to reach the mound on which the Pole stands". He went on to add that, "To arrive at the top when the hags are full of water is to have much of your pleasure spoilt". Not so today! What would he have thought of the stone pathway which now carries the 21st century walker with consummate ease over the final few hundred metres to 'the Pole's' huge concrete replacement?

4. Retrace your steps across the summit plateau and, when you reach the ladder stile **(GR NT914206)**, cross over and start your descent towards Scald Hill. The fence is now on your left. Heading rapidly downwards on a well-worn path, the temptation is to hurry. To do so, would be to miss the fine views to the Harthope Valley, the surrounding hills and beyond to the Northumberland coast. Immediately after a short, sometimes boggy, col a quick and easy climb brings you to the top of the 549 metre high Scald Hill. If W. Ford Robertson had been writing this particular walk he would have undoubtedly directed you to return to the valley by turning to your right before reaching Scald Hill and taking a route not too dissimilar to that of the 'permitted footpath' shown on the current edition of the Ordnance Survey 1: 25000 scale map. A steep, and in his own words "long and tedious" descent would eventually have brought you close to Langleeford Hope deep in the Harthope Valley. However, you are keeping to the high, open ground for as long as possible so that you can get the best of the views. So continue heading downhill and when, after a short while, the fence turns to the north **(GR NT933221)**, you need to bear to your right along a clear, rutted path heading in a generally easterly direction. To your right lies the second and third highest of the Cheviot Hills, the majestic Hedgehope Hill and the not quite so impressive Comb Fell joined together by a long peat hag-fringed ridge. Now it

Hedgehope Hill.

is just a simple matter of enjoying the rest of the descent along a clear path, with continuing views of the Harthope Valley laid out below you. Eventually, a short section of rough track will bring you to the tarmac valley road, a left hand turn and a gentle meander back to the Hawsen Burn. As you sit, soaking up the final moments of your `walk to the Pole`, having first splashed your face in the cool mountain water, thoughts of a hearty meal might just conceivably begin to slowly drift into your mind. On reaching the end of an outing into the Cheviot Hills, W. Ford Robertson told us that he experienced "an extraordinary relish for plain food" and enjoyed, "a sense of appreciation of the warmth and brightness of the supper room". He left us in no doubt whatsoever that, "the meal at the end of the day" was "essentially a part of the outing". With that in mind and with your taste buds well and truly tickled, it is now time to make tracks for home.

FGS Grading

Grading is F10 [D1, N2, T2, R2, H3]

Distance	1	6 – 12 miles
Navigation	2	Competent navigation skills needed
Terrain	2	25 -50% on graded track or path 50 – 75% off track
Remoteness	2	Countryside not in close proximity to habitation – less than 20% of the route within 2 miles
Height	3	Over 250 ft per mile

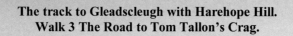

**The track to Gleadscleugh with Harehope Hill.
Walk 3 The Road to Tom Tallon's Crag.**

WALK 3: THE ROAD TO TOM TALLON`S CRAG

"There is a road", wrote W. Ford Robertson, "that runs over the eastern shoulder of Coldberry Hill and across Gains Law to the head of the Akeld Valley". "It is", he said, "for the most part level". Today, this "road" is a fine, green track which offers to those who venture westwards out of Wooler, a widescreen, high definition view towards the heart of the Cheviot Hills. This walk strides out across acres of windswept heather moor on its outward journey to the rocky outcrop viewpoint of Tom Tallon`s Crag. The return route chases the Akeld Burn downhill before following the northern edge of the Northumberland National Park back to Wooler. The views across Milfield Plain are outstanding.

DISTANCE: 9.25 miles (14.9 km)
ASCENT: 1330 feet (405 metres)
TERRAIN: Generally good paths and tracks, many of which are green, with the odd boggy patch. Two stretches of tarmac.
TIME: 4.5 hours
START: The Market Place, Wooler (GR NT993280)

Grid References

Wooler Market Place	993 280
Gate	972 275
Gains Law	956 281
Tom Tallon's Crag	933 281
Akeld Burn	952 289
Pond	972 285
Wooler Market Place	993 280

FGS Grading

Grading is F9 [D1, N2, T2, R2, H2]

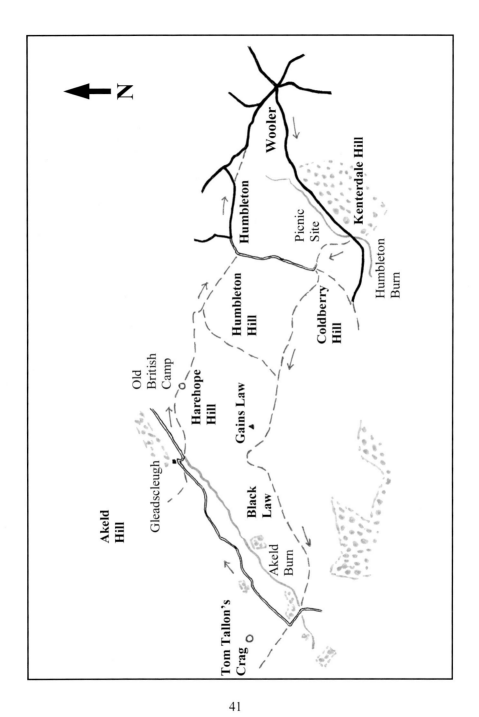

N

Wooler

Humbleton

Kenterdale Hill

Picnic Site

Humbleton Hill

Coldberry Hill

Humbleton Burn

Old British Camp

Harehope Hill

Gains Law

Gleadscleugh

Akeld Hill

Black Law

Akeld Burn

Tom Tallon's Crag

41

THE WALK

1. In the words of W. Ford Robertson, Wooler, "occupies a sheltered position on rising ground at the eastern edge of the Cheviot Hills". The Market Place is the most important public area in Wooler and, perhaps because of its elevated position, sloping topography and a high concentration of interesting buildings, it seems to define the essence of the town. From here, "the two main avenues to the hills" start their respective journeys. So, having parked your car in one of Wooler's car parks **(GR NT993280)**, it is time to begin your own journey by walking up Ramsey's Lane. Heading uphill, the narrow road soon becomes Common Road and, in 1926, the houses on the northern side did not exist. Followers of W. Ford Robertson's directions would, therefore, have had good views across open fields to the town below and maybe, if they were early risers, they would have caught a glimpse of the "9.25 a.m. train" puffing its way to Kirknewton Station. Stay with the road as it leaves the houses behind and continue on past the plantation-covered northern side of Kenterdale Hill. On reaching the Humbleton Burn Picnic Area, head across the car park and over the Humbleton Burn, via a small wooden footbridge. The clear footpath climbs up through a plantation, a relatively recent addition to the landscape. This area was referred to by W. Ford Robertson, as well as on maps of the area, as "The Targets" and was, during the 1914-18 World War, used as a rifle range. All traces of this former, less peaceful, use have long since disappeared. Once at the edge of the trees, pass through a small gate, called a "little gateway at the top of the brae" by W. Ford Robertson, and continue on until another gate is reached **(GR NT972275)**.

2. This is the "gateway" which "opens upon the Humbleton Common Road" and W. Ford Robertson instructed that "the direction is now over the north eastern shoulder of Coldberry Hill". So , turning left, continue along a fine, green track, following the route of the 62½ mile long St. Cuthbert's Way, a multi-day walk which links together the religious sites of Melrose Abbey and Lindisfarne. As you will now remain with this route until just prior to Tom Tallon's Crag, perhaps you will meet a passing 'pilgrim' along the way. The occasional 'Celtic Cross' way marker will keep you heading in the right direction. You are now contouring Coldberry Hill and, as you turn westwards across the "high moor", you will be greeted by an unfolding canvas containing some of the higher Cheviot Hills; Hedgehope Hill, Comb Fell, the Schil, Dunmoor Hill and, of course, The Cheviot itself. Soon you will pass, on your right, the imperceptible 319 metre high top of Gains Law **(GR NT956281)** and, if the mood should take you, a short diversion along a thin trace through cropped heather, will take you to the triangulation pillar -topped summit.

3. Continue, "around the head of the Glen between Gains Law and Black Law" and a quick scan of your Ordnance Survey map will reveal that this is the watershed of one of the many tiny tributaries of the Humbleton Burn. From here, W. Ford Robertson stated that, "the path curves around the eastern slope of Black Law to the corner of a wall" and then, "continues south westwards on the south eastern side of the wall". He added that at "a gate a little further on it crosses to the other side". The path is easy to follow as it heads, eventually over damp ground, in exactly the same direction as the 1926 version.

The track to Tom Tallon's Crag.

The small plantation to the right, at the other side of the Akeld Burn, is, however, a more modern addition to the moorland landscape. On reaching a near vertical ladder stile, which has replaced the rather more modest, "gate in the wall on the south side of the Knowe", it is time to bid farewell to St. Cuthbert's Way. Cross over the stile, turn right and follow the wall upwards for a short distance. As the crest of the path is reached, leave the wall behind and, turning to your left, walk the short distance to Tom Tallon's Crag **(GR NT933281)**. This splendid 353 metre high viewpoint makes an ideal place for a picnic. On picnics, like so many other subjects, W. Ford Robertson had some helpful advice. He suggested that "on the whole, it is best to leave the kettle behind" and advised instead "the vacuum flask" filled with "hot milk, coffee, cocoa or tea". He thought that some walkers might prefer "certain concentrated forms of food" such as "raisins and almonds, dates, ordinary chocolate and sanatogen chocolate". You will undoubtedly have your own personal well-tested 'secret' recipe for a day wandering in the hills.

Tom Tallon's Crag looking towards The Cheviot.

4. Time now to leave behind the expansive view and to retrace your steps, "as far as the track which rises along the north western bank of the Akeld Burn". This lies just before the small plantation passed on your outward journey. Once reached, turn left through a five bar gate and, with the Akeld Burn a short distance to your right, head downhill on a gravel track. The dark slopes of Harehope Hill rise away to the east and the double topped Akeld Hill dominates the skyline to the north as you begin to approach the buildings of Gleadscleugh.

Gleadscleugh with Akeld Hill behind.

At this point, W. Ford Robertson advised that "the track crosses the burn near Akeld Hill House (Gleadscleugh)" and then "skirts the south side of a field". So, be sure to follow the track, which cuts away from the main track to your right and, in a short distance, turns to cross the burn **(GR NT952289)**, situated in a pleasant little dene. Keep with the track as it begins to climb the lower slopes of Harehope Hill, following the field boundary uphill before turning eastwards and traversing the site of "an old British Camp". In a position enjoying extensive views of Milfield Plain, this was, in fact, a type of defended settlement of the early Iron Age, consisting of an enclosure contained within banks of earth and stone.

Akeld Hill from the "Old British Camp".

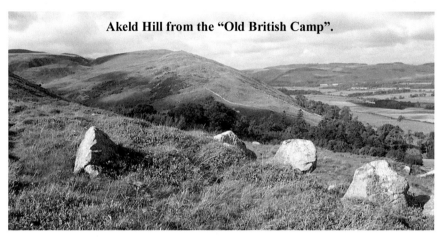

Once beyond the remnants of the settlement you will pass through a gate from which W. Ford Robertson said, "magnificent views may be obtained" and then, "at the head of Bendor Dene, a wicket gate". You will not be disappointed, the views are superb, although the two gates now have ladder stiles as close neighbours.

Humbleton Hill behind gate and stile.

5. Leaving behind the northern slopes of Harehope Hill, stay with the descending path as it takes aim for the rocky gap at the bottom of the slopes of Humbleton Hill. Go through the gap and, still with the main track, you will soon pass a small pond on your left **(GR NT972285)**. This was described as two "mill ponds" when W. Ford Robertson stopped here to admire the view.

The mill pond.

On reaching a gate alongside a foliage-invaded, tumbledown building, turn left and head downhill past a pretty cottage to your left, as far as the "village green" at the hamlet of Humbleton. The nearby telephone box would certainly not have stood here in 1926, a time when there were only 45 subscribers to the telephone service in the Wooler area. The pond, which had been at the centre of the "village green", has long since disappeared although the ground alongside the road remains exceedingly wet. Turn right and continue down the hawthorn hedge lined lane, and, on reaching the bend, heed the advice of W. Ford Robertson and take a short cut, "by a path across a field". On joining the road, turn right past the magnificent stag-adorned entrance to the Highburn House Caravan Park, and head towards Wooler. Soon you will pass the 1856-built St. Ninian`s Church which, in 1926, would have marked the extreme north-western edge of the town. From here it is all gently downhill to the car park where you left your car a few hours ago. As you peel off your outer, mid and base layers of clothing, feeling at the top of your game, bear a thought for the "patients who used to flock to the town to drink goat`s whey" in the 19[th] century, long before the original `Walks from Wooler` was published in 1926. One such patient who came to

Wooler, looking for an improvement to her health, was none other than North-umberland's own lifeboat heroine Grace Darling. Sadly, she was to die less than one year later.

FGS Grading

Grading is F9 [D1, N2, T2, R2, H2]

Distance	1	6 – 12 miles
Navigation	2	Competent navigation skills needed
Terrain	2	50 – 75% on graded track or path 25 – 50% off track
Remoteness	2	Countryside not in close proximity to habitation – less than 20% of the route within 2 miles
Height	2	Over 125 ft per mile

From the moor above the Hellpath.
Walk 4. The Hart Heugh Glidders.

WALK 4: THE HART HEUGH GLIDDERS

Described in W. Ford Robertson's book as flowing through "a rocky and rugged valley", the Carey Burn is a mere 1½ miles in length. The steep northern side of the narrow, twisting valley is dominated by the glidder-shattered, gorse-embellished slopes of the 326 metre high Hart Heugh, a hill with an outstanding view. This walk starts in the centre of Wooler and follows a long-neglected route to the Carey Burn via Kenterdale Hill, Earlehillhead and Switcherdown. It then stalks the Carey Burn as far as the delightful Hellpath before visiting the tops of Hart Heugh and Brown's Law on the winding way back to Wooler.

DISTANCE: 8.25 miles (13.3 km)
ASCENT: 1263 feet (385 metres)
TERRAIN: Generally good paths and tracks, many of which are green. Some stretches of tarmac.
TIME: 4 hours
START: The Market Place, Wooler (GR NT993280)

Grid References

Market Place	993 280
Waud House	984 276
Metal gate	975 265
Metal gate	976 256
Finger post	958 257
Hart Heugh	968 255
Common Road	972 270
Brown's Law	973 272
Market Place	993 280

FGS Grading

Grading is F8 [D1, N2, T1, R2, H2]

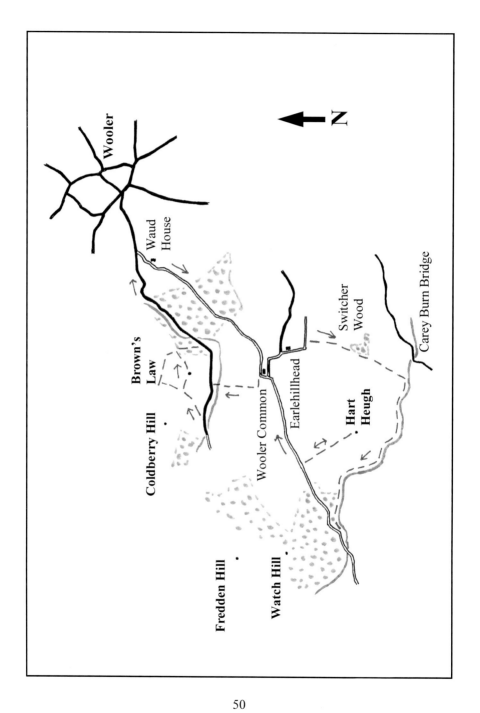

THE WALK

1. When `Walks from Wooler` was published in the year of the General Strike, there were two banks in Wooler, "the British Linen in the Market Place and the Bank of Liverpool and Martins Ltd in the High Street". The town was also "well served by the Alnwick and Coldstream Branch of the London and North-Eastern Railway". Today, visitors to the stone-built streets will find a different range of facilities to tickle their fancy. Park your car in one of town`s car parks, head for the Market Place **(GR NT993280)** and "leave Wooler by Ramsey`s Lane". As you climb up the lower part of the lane, watch out for two buildings of particular interest, the first of which is on the left hand side. This building, and attached garages, was once used as stables and carriage sheds and was erected in the late 18th or early 19th century. Sadly, this is currently in a sorry state of repair. Slightly higher up, on the right hand side, stands number 18, a property built in the early years of the 17th century. Both buildings are Grade II Listed. Soon the narrow lane becomes Common Road and the various houses to your right are a post-1926 addition to the `streetscene` and, when W. Ford Robertson passed this way he urged walkers, "to stop and look back in order to enjoy the fine view of the town and country beyond". Just prior to the end of the row of houses, a sign-post on the opposite side of the road, indicating `Public Bridleway Wooler Common 1`, points your way ahead. Cross over the road and turn left along the gravel track.

The track to Waud House.

2. You are heading towards Waud House **(GR NT984276)** which you will, in due course, pass on your left. This is in fact a `pretty as a picture` whitewashed stone cottage in an idyllic setting. This area has changed somewhat since W. Ford Robertson noted that, "Just beyond the house, you enter on the Golf Course, which extends mainly over Kenterdale Hill lying before you".

The whitewashed Waud House.

The Golf Course is no more and a substantial part of Kenterdale Hill is now covered with trees. You are now following the route of St. Cuthbert`s Way, heading in the direction of a distant Melrose, so for the next short stretch of the walk you will have the occasional Celtic Cross adorned directional fingerpost as your guide. The route heads away from Waud House, passing through a small gate signed `Public Footpath Pin Well ½` and then, in quick succession, a second small gate. Once through, turn left and after less than 100 metres, where there is a dip in the hillside, turn right and follow the path which bends left uphill. Soon you will reach a directional fingerpost and, looking around you, it is easy to imagine the attractions of a `round of golf` on this hillside with a view. Continue in the same direction and, with the plantation straight ahead, aim for the left hand gate. Go through the gate and keep with the path as it works its way through the plantation. When the path splits in two, be sure to take the left hand, downhill fork. Before long you will, once again, emerge into daylight. Passing through a single wooden gate, your route continues slightly left with another plantation on the far horizon and the buildings of Earlehillhead away to your left. Eventually, a directional fingerpost indicates that St. Cuthbert`s Way turns to the right and, at this point, it is time to say farewell to this `northern pilgrim`s way`. Continue straight on until you are, as W. Ford Robertson described, "within sight of Reastead" and a quick glance at your Ordnance Survey map will show that the buildings you can see ahead are those of `Wooler Common`. You are not, however, lost. At some time after 1926 `Reastead` underwent a change of name and the former name is now all but forgotten.

3. Keep with the dry stone wall on your left as far as a metal gate **(GR NT975265)** and an adjoining signpost pointing the way to Broadstruther. Here you must turn left along a gravel track which, after dropping slightly downhill, meets with a tarmac road. This eventually leads to Earle, a road you must ignore. Stay with the track as it bends to the right and climbs uphill past the quiet Earlehillhead, on your left. On reaching the large barn at the top of the hill, turn left and then, after passing through a metal gate, turn immediately right. Now head across the cropped-grass field on a faint track, with the unmistakeable Hedgehope Hill straight ahead in the far distance. To your right, the craggy Hart Heugh, a hill you will climb later in the walk, peeps over the tree tops. The route you are following was regularly utilised by W. Ford Robertson but, possibly as a consequence of there having been no public right of way, it seems to have been neglected in recent years. However, in January 2008, Northumberland County Council made and confirmed a `footpath modification order` which, in a nutshell, created a new public right of way running from Wooler Common to the Carey Burn, along the route you are now travelling. After passing through another metal gate the green track heads downhill with a secondary and fainter track soon bending to the right, towards the right-hand edge of Switcher Wood. Follow this secondary track, crossing first a large wooden gate and then yet another metal gate **(GR NT976256)**. Once over the second gate, aim for the solitary tree some 200 metres ahead.

The lonely tree at Switcherdown.

In 1926, Switcher Wood did not exist and, in his book, W. Ford Robertson indicated that, "you will see a clump of elm and ash trees and a ruin". He went on to explain, "This is Switcherdown, where tradition says there once dwelt a witch". He said that he knew people, "who allege that at dusk they have seen her ghost, still haunting the place". He described the scene, saying, "a fine view may be obtained of the lower part of the Harthope Valley, of Langlee Crags and Housey Crags, and of Hedgehope towering in the distance". Indeed there is a fine view with the added ingredients of Snear Hill and the `topknot` of Cold Law. Beside your feet lie the bare bones of Switcherdown, but what remains of the witch? If you are interested perhaps you should follow the advice of W. Ford Robertson and, "make a late evening visit".

4. Continue your journey downhill, keeping the dry stone wall close to your left -hand side. As you near the bottom of the hill, cross over the five bar gate and continue into the valley of the Carey Burn, following the fine, green track as it bends upstream, to your right. To your left, some 200 metres away, a just visible 1956-built, white balustrade-edged bridge straddles the burn near the point where it merges with the Harthope Burn. Continue up the increasingly narrow and rocky valley. The skinny path cuts across the `glidders` of Hart Heugh before reaching a series of small, but nonetheless impressive, waterfalls. The main waterfall was referred to by W. Ford Robertson as, "Careyburn Linn" and "a favourite spot for picnics". He added, perhaps with a hint of understatement, that, "the waterfall is quite a good subject for the camera".

Careyburn Linn.

Continue with the burn and the narrow path passing, as the valley bends to the west, a small open wooden shelter and then the southern, tree-fringed slopes of Watch Hill. Before long, beside a directional fingerpost **(GR NT958257)**, the path merges with a good, green track which continues upstream. However, your route turns sharp right up the steep track known as the Hellpath.

The start of the Hellpath.

The name is said to be a corruption of `hill path` but, as you climb steadily up-hill with great views to the valley below, you may just feel that the name has a more literal meaning. Soon you will leave the trees behind, emerging onto the open moor with Watch Hill and Fredden Hill to your left and Hart Heugh, your next objective, to your right. Continue straight on along a track with a firm base and after some 300 metres you will see a subsidiary track on your right. This is your out and back route to the summit of Hart Heugh.

5. So, turn to your right and, when reached, go through the five bar gate. Keep straight ahead and when you are parallel with the rocky top of the hill, leave the track behind and head to your right across pathless grassland to reach the 326 metre high summit **(GR NT968255)**.

This is capped with a large and rambling pile of stones which provides excellent shelter from the often present wind. If the weather is fine, this is a perfect place to tuck into the sandwiches. On the subject of picnics, W. Ford Robertson seems to have been well-versed. In his `Hints to the Pedestrian` he said, "The old picnic fire and kettle are nowadays generally superseded by a vacuum flask". Whilst he understood that, "Much time and trouble are undoubtedly thereby saved", he felt that, "not a little pleasure is lost, except in damp weather, when available fuel is not in a state to burn". This hill enjoys a princely view and, looking west, from left to right you can see Dunmoor Hill, Hedgehope Hill, Cold Law, The Cheviot, Preston Hill, Newton Tors and more besides. Return to the track across the moor along the way you came.

The view from Hart Heugh.

6. Once on the track, turn right and continue your walk in a north-easterly direction. Soon you will pass a plantation to your right, as you begin to head downhill towards the buildings of Wooler Common. The gravel track makes for easy walking and, on reaching the buildings, cross the step stile on your left, signposted `Brown`s Law ¼ Wooler 1¾`. On the opposite side of the small field, cross over another step stile, turn left and follow the green track westwards, signposted ` Brown`s Law ¼`. The track quickly turns to the north, tumbling downhill alongside a tributary of the Humbleton Burn. At the bottom of the hill, the track fords the shallow tributary and then, almost immediately, the slightly deeper Humbleton Burn. If you prefer to be more sedate, you have the option of

Crossing the Humbleton Burn.

crossing the burn via a small wooden footbridge which bears a tiny plaque inscribed, `In memory of Stanley Bell 1916-1991 Who loved these hills`. A short climb delivers you to the `Common Road` **(GR NT972270)**. The gorse covered flanks of Brown`s Law lie straight ahead and the top of this 237 metre high hill is your next target.

The summit of Brown's Law.

Turn left along the thin tarmac road and after 400 metres of walking, just as the road begins to descend to the bridge over the Humbleton Burn, leave the road behind. Pass through a five bar gate on your right, next to a signpost indicating 'Public Footpath Humbleton 1', turn sharp right and head uphill on a clear green path as far as the saddle between Coldberry Hill, to your left, and Brown's Law, on your right.

7. Pass through the five bar gate, beside which there is a convenient seat, turn immediately to your right and pass through another five bar gate. Now head straight uphill making the short climb to the cairn-marked summit of Brown's Law **(GR NT973272)**. This is a fantastic 360° viewpoint of the surrounding countryside. You will be able to pick out Kenterdale Hill, Hart Heugh, The Cheviot, Cold Law, Hedgehope Hill, Watch Hill, Fredden Hill, Newton Tors, Coldberry Hill and Humbleton Hill as well as Wooler and Milfield Plain. Leave the summit by following the dilapidated dry stone wall downhill over bracken-covered slopes towards the corner of a plantation and, when you reach a green path, turn left as far as a small gate on your right. You have, once again, joined hands with St. Cuthbert's Way. Go through the gate and head downwards through the trees, eventually reaching the Humbleton Burn and the adjoining picnic area. Cross over the wooden footbridge and head to your right, across the car park, to join the tarmac road below the plantation covered slopes of Kenterdale Hill. You are back on the 'Common Road' and, by turning to your left, you will start the final 1¼ miles back to Wooler. Now simply enjoy the gentle, generally downhill, walk. You will eventually rejoin your outward route at the point where you left the road for Waud House and, "if some members of the party are beginning to flag", just follow the advice of W. Ford Robertson and "start singing a march". As he said, "Most vocalists will have a few in their repertoire".

FGS Grading

Grading is F8 [D1, N2, T1, R2, H2]

Distance	1	6 – 12 miles
Navigation	2	Competent navigation skills needed
Terrain	1	50 – 75% on graded track or path 25 – 50% off track
Remoteness	2	Countryside not in close proximity to habitation – less than 20% of the route within 2 miles
Height	2	Over 125 ft per mile

St Cuthbert's Way towards the College Valley.
Walk 5 High Above the College Burn.

WALK 5: HIGH ABOVE THE COLLEGE BURN

Formed by a geological fault, the College Valley penetrates southwards from Glendale, deep into the Cheviot Hills. It is considered by many to be the finest valley in the county. "The scenery of the College is extremely pretty", wrote W. Ford Robertson with a hint of understatement, and it is, undoubtedly, at its most beautiful in Spring when the bright yellow gorse is in full flower. On this walk you will follow the ruler-straight valley from Hethpool to the farmstead of Southernknowe, before turning briefly into the remote Lambden Valley. You will then climb high onto the hills which rise to the east and where spectacular views of the valley and the border hills beyond await. This is a walk to devour.

DISTANCE: 9.75 miles (15.7 km)
ASCENT: 1362 feet (415 metres)
TERRAIN: Mainly clear paths and tracks, some quite rough, and a stretch of tarmac
TIME: 5 hours
START: Hethpool, College Valley (GR NT893280)

Grid References

Hethpool	893 280
Sutherland Bridge	888 249
Signpost	890 244
Fence	905 254
Hare Law	902 265
Newton Tors	908 269
Easter Tor	915 281
Track junction	916 291
Bridge	902 285
Hethpool	893 280

FGS Grading

Grading is F9 [D1, N2, T2, R2, H2]

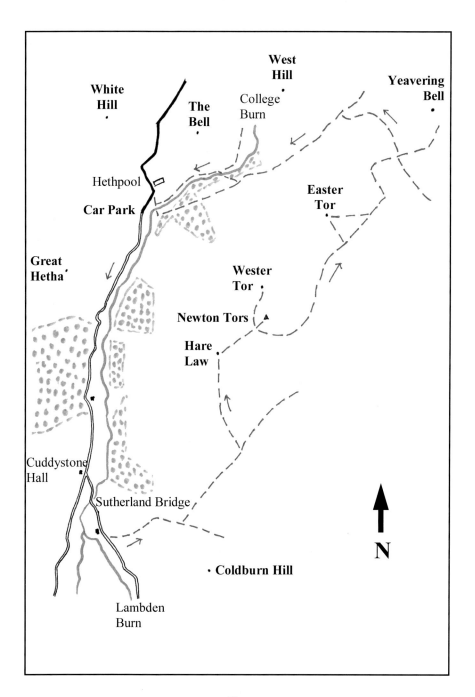

White
Hill

West
Hill

Yeavering
Bell

The
Bell

College
Burn

Hethpool

Easter
Tor

Car Park

Great
Hetha

Wester
Tor

Newton Tors

Hare
Law

Cuddystone
Hall

Sutherland Bridge

Coldburn Hill

Lambden
Burn

N

THE WALK

1. The 7½ mile road journey from Wooler to Hethpool in the College Valley hugs the edge of the Cheviot Hills and follows closely the course of the former 35½ mile long Alnwick to Cornhill Branch Railway. Opened to passengers in 1887, the line possessed some of the finest railway station buildings ever constructed on a rural branch line. When making tracks for Hethpool, W. Ford Robertson recommended that you, "take the morning train to Kirknewton Station", and, as you head towards the starting point of this walk, be sure to watch out for the former stone-built station buildings which stand on the right hand side of the road between Kirknewton and Westnewton. The buildings of Hethpool lie along a signposted, unclassified single track road heading southwards off the B6351. There is a small parking area just beyond the hamlet, immediately after a cattle grid **(GR NT893280)** . Perfectly parked, now it is time to slip your trusty `guide to the great outdoors global positioning system` into your back pocket, to take a final bite of your cranberry and maple syrup carbohydrate-loaded cereal bar and to start your day by heading south along the narrow valley road. When heading this way, back in the 1920`s, W. Ford Robertson referred to "the cart road that leads up the glen" and, whilst the surface of the present road has been improved since then it is, by no means, billiard-table smooth. Public vehicular access through the valley is restricted to 12 cars per day and, as a consequence, you should be relatively untroubled by traffic as you make your switchback way, surrounded by glorious hills.

Memorial to Allied airmen near Cuddystone Hall.

2. On your left rise the rugged Newton Tors, whilst the rounded slopes of the Iron Age hillfort-topped Great Hetha climb away to your right. Soon the tree-covered Sinkside Hill is brushed past on your right and then the buildings of Whitehall, downhill towards the burn. After a further ½ mile of walking, with the huge bulk of The Cheviot now dominating the valley, it is time to head towards Southernknowe and the Lambden Valley by taking the road to your left. Standing next to the junction is Cuddystone Hall, the educational, cultural and social centre of the valley. Nearby is a memorial to the allied airmen who lost their lives in the Cheviots between 1939 and 1945. A signpost indicating `Southernknowe ½ Goldscleugh 2½` points the way ahead and, before you have time to get into your stride, the College Burn is crossed via Sutherland Bridge **(GR NT888249)**.

The College Burn beside Sutherland Bridge.

Alternatively, if you wish to splash your boots, the concrete base of the adjacent ford offers a slightly more challenging route. In the 1926 book `Walks from Wooler` this was merely, " a foot-bridge by which you must cross the College Water" which stood, "a quarter of a mile below Southernknowe, the hill farm at the foot of the Lambden Burn". The single storey buildings of Southernknowe enjoy an elevated position and as you head onwards you will, in the words of W. Ford Robertson, "Continue past the north side of Southernknowe and follow the road up the Lambden Glen". You are now nearly 2½ miles into your journey and, after a further 100 metres of walking, it is time to head for higher ground.

3. On the left hand side of the road a public footpath **(GR NT890244)**, signpost-ed `Commonburn House 3`, climbs up the steep grass-covered eastern side of the valley and W. Ford Robertson described this as the path which, "starts from the Dunsdale road", and "ascends the steep and long slope as a peat-cart road". So, take a deep breath and begin your 2 mile upward journey. As you begin to climb, the views behind you to The Cheviot and the cleft of The Bizzle are par-ticularly impressive. Eventually, when the gradient begins to ease, the path splits in two so be sure to take the right hand spur as you continue your tramp across the wide expanse of heather moor. To your right lies Coldburn Hill and, despite the huge presence of The Cheviot behind you, there is a sense of infinite space. At a directional fingerpost bear left and on reaching a five bar gate cross over and head straight on for 300 metres. At this point, leave the main track and follow the rougher track on your right passing eventually the remains of an old stone enclosure. Soon, with 1¼ miles under your belt since leaving "the Duns-dale road" and more than 210 metres of ascent in your legs you will arrive at a post and wire fence, cutting across the moor on a north-west/south-east course **(GR NT905254)**. Your route heads towards the north-west, so, turning to your left, continue on your journey and, after a further ¾ mile of relatively easy, alt-hough occasionally damp, walking, the cairn-capped top of Hare Law **(GR NT902265)** is reached. At a height of 518 metres, the stone-strewn summit of-fers one of the best seats in the Cheviot house. The College Valley stretches out way below you surrounded by a multitude of admiring hills; the Schil, Black Hag, Saughieside Hill, Loft Hill, Blackhaggs Rigg and, of course, The Cheviot, with the hillside-splitting cleft of the Bizzle and the skyward-pointing Braydon Crag particularly eye-catching. This is more or less the half-way point of the

Blackhaggs Rigg from Hare Law.

walk and, with the views difficult to leave, these dizzy heights make the perfect spot for a bite to eat. The subject of picnics occupied a place close to W. Ford Robertson's heart and, when offering "Hints to the Pedestrian" on the thorny question of what to drink whilst out and about, he noted that some people, "advocate cold tea without milk in a common flask". Perhaps expressing a more personal preference, he went on to add that, "many prefer to fill this with something stronger of the same colour". Now there is an idea!

4. Now head back to the corner of the dry stone wall and the adjacent directional fingerpost which you passed on first reaching the summit. Turn left and, with the fence-hugging path and the stone wall to your right, walk to the next step stile. Climb over, head up the short slope and on reaching a track, turn left as far as a shin-high directional sign. Turn to face the sign and angling slightly to your left strike out across heather-covered ground to the triangulation pillar marking the top of Newton Tors **(GR NT908269)**. Keep an eye out for the occasional peat pool. Standing at a height of 537 metres, this is the highest point of the walk, although not the best viewpoint.

Newton Tors summit.

Leave the heather-clad top by heading in a north-westerly direction and, on reaching a green track, follow this to your right as far as the obvious Wester Tor. From this rocky promontory there are splendid views across the College Valley to the green, rolling border hills and the North Sea coast where, on a clear day, Lindisfarne can just be seen . Your next objective, Easter Tor, lies to the north-east and is reached by heading back along the track you have just

The view from Wester Tor.

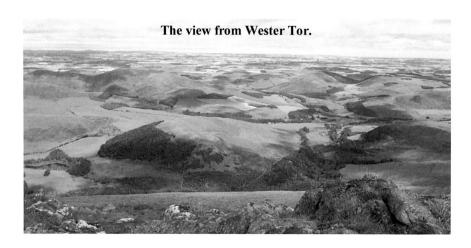

come. Stay with this track as bends around Newton Tors and, as you stroll happily across the moor watch out for the shy feral goats which have roamed this part of Northumberland for centuries. Eventually, as you begin to approach Easter Tor, you will need to leave the main track by turning to your left signposted `Easter Tor ¼`. An easy walk will rapidly deliver you onto the 438 metre high rocky top **(GR NT915281)** where once again there are fine views, especially of the impressively rugged profile of Wester Tor.

Yeavering Bell from Easter Tor.

5. Leave the top by taking the footpath signed `Yeavering Bell 1½` and, in a short while, you will rejoin the track across the moor beside a 3-fingered shin high directional sign. Turn left and, after 100 metres, turn left again heading downhill through a mixture of grass and heather. As you go, take time to admire the fine views towards the College Valley and the tiny settlement of Hethpool, your ultimate destination. As your route reaches more even ground the track bends to the right and begins to contour the lower hillside. The occasional directional marker post will keep you heading in the right direction. In turn, you will pass a five bar gate on your left. Do not go through. Keep straight on and very quickly you will see a ladder stile taking a giant step across a dry stone wall. Beyond lies Yeavering Bell. Cross over the stile and join a green track and the route of St. Cuthbert's Way which, to your right, heads towards a distant Wooler and then, eventually, to the North Sea coast and Lindisfarne. Your route, which also follows St. Cuthbert's Way but in the opposite direction, turns to the left on a gradual downhill course. On reaching another ladder stile, climb over and stay with the green track as it continues to run downhill as far as the junction **(GR NT916291)** with a gravel track. Away to your right and out of sight lies the tiny settlement of Old Yeavering, which consists of two mid-19th century cottages and an old farm outbuilding dating back to at least 1584.

6. Now, with just 2 miles of ground to cover, your route turns to the left and heads the short distance to Torleehouse. Once past the buildings, keep walking in the same direction passing through a small plantation before heading downhill, with Easter Tor looming large on one side and the appropriately named hill, The Bell rising from the opposite banks of the College Burn on the other side. Spread across the western slopes of this 247 metre high hill are the oak trees of Hethpoolbell Wood, planted by Admiral Lord Collingwood, Nelson's second in

The Bell from St Cuthbert's Way.

command at the Battle of Trafalgar and a former resident of Hethpool Manor.

Eventually, you will pass a square stone sheepfold on your right before crossing into a gorse-filled dip via a step stile. Do not exit the dip at the next step stile. Instead turn right on a thin yellow arrow marked path and head downwards to the gated bridge over the College Burn **(GR NT902285)**. You are now within sight of Hethpool Linn, " a favourite spot" for picnics , although, wrote W. Ford Robertson , "a little dangerous for children". Admire the linn from the centre of the bridge. Now, cross over the bridge, turn left and continue above the burn, keeping close to the post and wire fence and the stone wall. Cross over a small bridge and, in quick succession, a step stile. Continue onwards along a clear path with a post and wire fence to your right. When this bends upwards, keep straight on, crossing the small stream via a wooden bridge. Now aim for the gate in the stone wall and then head towards a step stile at the far side of the small field. Cross over, turn to your right on a rough, rising track and after passing through yet another gate turn left onto the valley road. Now it is a simple matter of walking past the delightful row of four 1926-built `Arts and Crafts` style cottages, stepping over the cattle grid and then, back at the small parking area, bundling your sweat-soaked lightweight walking gear into the boot of your car. At a time when the mass produced, assembly-line motor car had still to make an impact on the lives of ordinary folk, W. Ford Robertson wrote in his 1926-published book, "Yet it is certain that, for those in whom modern civilisation, with its elaborate provision for rapid locomotion, has not entirely destroyed the capacity for enjoying a country walk, the district can offer rich, and in some respects unique delights". Little did he realise the changes in "rapid locomotion" that the next 80 years or so would bring to an ever-evolving world.

FGS Grading

Grading is F9 [D1, N2, T2, R2, H2]

Distance	1	6 – 12 miles
Navigation	2	Competent navigation skills needed
Terrain	2	25 -50% on graded track or path 50 – 75% off / single track
Remoteness	2	Countryside not in close proximity to habitation – less than 20% of the route within 2 miles
Height	2	Over 125 ft per mile

The track from Langlee Crags towards Housey Crags.
Walk 6 The Eastern Fringe.

WALK 6: THE EASTERN FRINGE

Lying on the eastern edge of the Northumberland National Park overlooking the entrance to the Harthope Valley, Brands Hill occupies an outstanding position. "In clear weather, fine views are obtainable from the top", promised W. Ford Robertson and suggested three different routes to the summit. This walk finds its own way to the high ground of Brands Hill and then, after admiring the view, makes tracks towards the pretty and attractively located cottage of Middleton Dean. Turning to head for home, the route then visits the spectacular outcrops of Middleton and Langlee Crags before making a dramatic return to the Harthope Valley.

DISTANCE: 6.5 miles (10.5 km)
ASCENT: 1115 feet (340 metres)
TERRAIN: Mainly good, clear tracks and paths throughout
TIME: 3.5 hours
START: Near Langlee, Harthope Valley (GR NT963233)

Grid References

Near Langlee, Harthope Valley	963 233
Green track	974 237
Gate	993 223
Langlee Crags	966 221
Near Langlee, Harthope Valley	963 233

FGS Grading

Grading is F8 [D1, N2, T1, R2, H2]

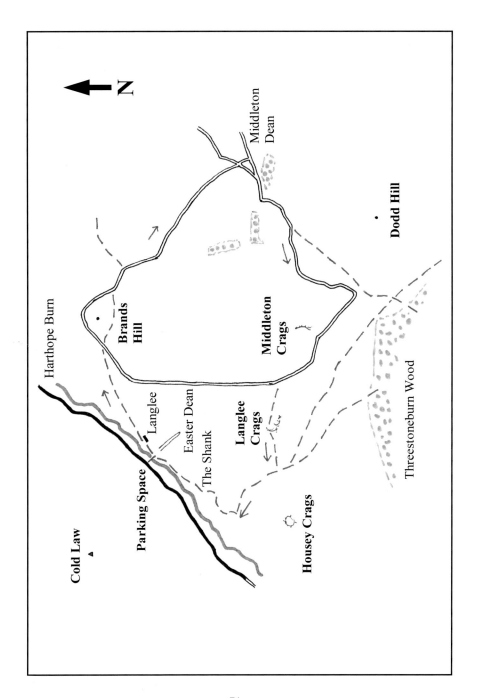

N

Middleton Dean

Dodd Hill

Harthope Burn

Brands Hill

Middleton Crags

Threestoneburn Wood

Langlee

Easter Dean

The Shank

Langlee Crags

Cold Law

Parking Space

Housey Crags

71

THE WALK

1. "Having settled on your route, you are off, on a bright summer morning", wrote W. Ford Robertson and, as you drive along the winding, single track road from Wooler to your starting point near Langlee, 1¼ miles along the beautiful Harthope Valley, your expectations of a fine day in the hills will be high. The former shepherd's cottage of Langlee stands, "at the foot of Easter Dean", on the south-eastern side of the valley and enjoys superb elevated views. There are parking places on the grass **(GR NT963233)** alongside the valley road within sight of the cottage. Once out into the open air and having checked your computer-generated route elevation profile and projected journey time, slipped on your three-season fabric trekking boots with state-of-the-art waterproof and breathable membrane and packed your essential supply of raisins, peanuts, jelly beans and, of course, a slab of Kendal Mint Cake you are now ready for the off! Back in the 1920's, W. Ford Robertson instructed the walker to, "cross the Harthope Burn by the footbridge" and, whilst this is now a rather more substantial bailey bridge, this is your direction of travel, with a helpful signpost, alongside a cattle grid and step stile, pointing the way to `Middleton Old Town 1¾. North Middleton 2¾`.

Near Langlee - the start.

72

2. Once across the delightful burn and standing next to a second signpost, you will be staring straight into the mouth of Easter Dean, hillside-splitting and something of a gem. "For those who are fond of a climbing adventure", said W. Ford Robertson, "a scramble up the Easter Dean may be thrown in, but most people", he noted, "will be content to view this chasm from the top of one or other bank". Elsewhere in his book, he warned the more intrepid walker that Easter Dean will, "if he is not careful, readily provide his heirs with a reason for realising his life insurance policy". A sobering thought at the beginning of your walk!

Easter Dean.

Your route turns to the left, signposted 'Old Middleton 2', and follows a stone track towards and then along a thin path in front of the buildings of Langlee. From here a grass track climbs across the slopes of Brands Hill and, as you head steadily upwards, first-class views begin to open up. Directly to your left, Cold Law rises sharply from the valley floor, whilst behind you the thread-thin Harthope Burn leads the eye towards its source, high on Scotsman's Knowe, where Hedgehope Hill and the mighty Cheviot vie for attention. Eventually, the gradient begins to ease and, when a green track with a firm stone base **(GR NT974237)** is reached, you will need to leave behind the public footpath you

Hedgehope Hill and The Cheviot.

have been following since the valley and to turn to your left. This track, which will be your guide for the next 1¾ miles to Middleton Dean, initially heads in a north-easterly direction and when, in time, you arrive at a five bar gate, turn to your right and head the short distance to the 319 metre high top of the heather-covered Brands Hill.

3. As you stand here high above the place where the Harthope and Carey Burns collide, merging to form Coldgate Water, the panorama stretches out across the Cheviot foothills to Wooler and beyond. "Every intelligent person who visits this district must be struck by the large number of old `camps` that he sees in the course of his walk", wrote W. Ford Robertson, adding that, "There are at least five on the north-eastern slopes of Brands Hill". He was, of course, referring to the settlements, which consisted of hut circles surrounded by banks of earth and stones, that made up a Roman period village (AD 43-AD 410). These settle-ments, and many of the other ancient remains scattered around this particular area, are Scheduled Ancient Monuments under the Ancient Monuments and Archaeological Areas Act 1979 and it is a criminal offence to damage any such monument. Return back to the track and pass through the five bar gate. Continue to follow the firm track as it gently descends in a south-easterly direction, with the settlements of Middleton Old Town, North Middleton and South Middleton lying away to your left. Soon the track levels and the grasslands climb gently to your right as you confidently stride out towards Middleton Dean. Keep a sharp eye peeled for this area is a favoured habitat of the hare. Eventually, just beyond the fourth five bar gate **(GR NT993223)** since leaving the summit of Brands

Hill, a public footpath arriving from South Middleton steps across the post and wire fence and heads diagonally to your right. This is your route, but first you should head straight on for some 200 metres. Downhill lies the bonny cottage of Middleton Dean, perfectly situated above one of the tributaries of the Lilburn Burn, surrounded by gorse-flecked banks and seemingly served by more than its fair share of tracks and public footpaths.

Middleton Dean and the banks of gorse.

Head back to the stile, step over and cut diagonally across the field to join a track running alongside a small plantation. Stay with this track for the next 1¼ miles as it heads in a generally south-westerly direction, contouring the lower slopes of Middleton Crags, towards Threestoneburn Wood, a large plantation which sweeps up the east facing flanks of Hedgehope Hill and Dunmoor Hill. You will enjoy a sense of immense space.

4. Eventually a clear but occasionally damp track, which begins to climb towards Middleton Crags, will invite you to turn right. Accept the invitation and, when parallel with the 404 metre high crags, leave the track and spend a wee while exploring the rocky promontory. Back in the 1920's the slopes of Dunmoor Hill and Hedgehope Hill were not covered by the swathe of Threestoneburn Wood and the visitor to these rocky heights would have had clear views to the now tree-enveloped 18th century Threestoneburn House, a Grade II Listed

Middleton Crags.

Building. After enjoying the far reaching views, particularly to the south where Cunyan Crags can be seen peering over the tree tops, go back to the track and continue in the same direction as you were heading. When this track cuts through a series of 10 wooden shooting butts, turn left behind these butts and head towards the obvious Langlee Crags, a short distance ahead. The going can be particularly heavy, especially after prolonged rain. The crags cover a fairly extensive area of ground so be sure to make your way to the two most prominent crags **(GR NT966221)** lying to the north. After carefully scrambling to the top you will see for yourself that the views towards the Harthope Valley and westwards to The Cheviot and Hedgehope Hill are outstanding. It is just possible that they are also the best views you are likely to get of these two iconic hills from anywhere in the county. The Northumberland coast, to the east, can be spotted by a keen eye on a clear day.

5. Now, perhaps a little reluctantly, leave Langlee Crags via a thin sheep trace which heads westwards, in the general direction of Housey Crags. Soon you will meet up with a quad track. Turn right, continue as far as a good firm track and then take a moment to glance back towards Langlee Crags. You will now see them at their very best. Once done, turn to your left and walk as far as a five bar gate. Do not go through. You need to follow the public bridleway which rapidly marches downhill on a clear, green track. Soon the deepening cleft of Wester Dean will be on your right and, eventually, as the fence bends to the left, away

Langlee Crags and a distant Cheviot.

from the dean, the bridleway turns to the right and, passing a perfectly formed circular stone sheep stell, follows a small ridge known as the Shank.

A perfectly formed sheep stell.

The Harthope Burn is now just a little way below you, on your left, and from this point it is now a pleasant stroll back to the bridge across the burn, "at the foot of Easter Dean", and to the comfort of your car. As you contentedly prepare

The bridleway across The Shank.

for your journey home, perhaps you will be thinking, as did W. Ford Robertson, that, "Some kind soul knowing, far better than you did when you set out in the morning, how hungry and thirsty you would be when you returned will almost certainly have provided amply for your needs". Well, you can but dream!

FGS Grading

Grading is F8 [D1, N2, T1, R2, H2]

Distance	1	6 – 12 miles
Navigation	2	Competent navigation skills needed
Terrain	1	50 – 75% on graded track or path 25 – 50% off track
Remoteness	2	Countryside not in close proximity to habitation – less than 20% of the route within 2 miles
Height	2	Over 125 ft per mile

Heading down the Harthope Valley.
Walk 7 From Valley Floor to Summit Cairn.

WALK 7: FROM VALLEY FLOOR TO SUMMIT CAIRN

"Choose a clear day", suggested W. Ford Robertson, "because your chief objective must be to enjoy the magnificent distant views that may, under conditions of good visibility, be enjoyed from the top". At 714 metres in height, Hedgehope Hill is the second highest of the Cheviot Hills and is, perhaps, the most elegant. It is separated from the mighty Cheviot by the wild, upper reaches of the beautiful Harthope Valley. This walk visits two of the area's most popular crags, climbs the steep, north-eastern slopes of Hedgehope Hill and crosses the lonely ridge to Comb Fell. It then runs for home alongside the infant Harthope Burn.

DISTANCE: 8.25 miles (13.3 km)
ASCENT: 1952 feet (595 metres)
TERRAIN: Mainly clear, thin paths over sometimes rough and boggy ground. A stretch of gravel track and tarmac road.
TIME: 5 hours
START: Hawsen Burn, Harthope Valley (GR NT953225)

Grid References

Hawsen Burn	953 225
Stile	956 213
Hedgehope Hill	943 197
Comb Fell	924 187
Fingerpost	906 190
Langleeford Hope	932 207
Hawsen Burn	953 225

FGS Grading

Grading is F9 [D1, N2, T2, R2, H2]

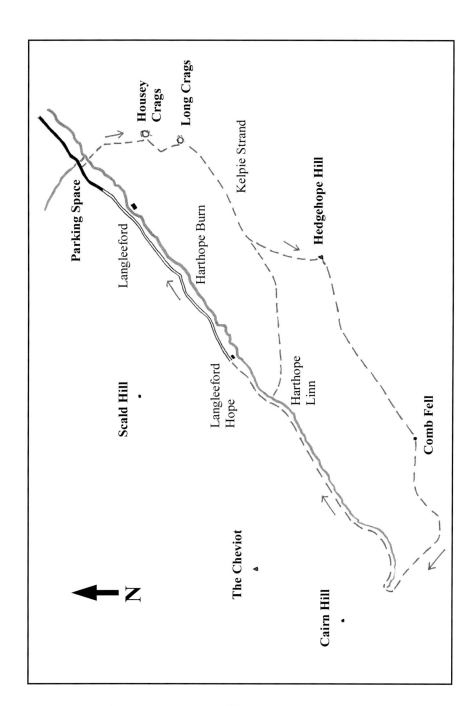

N

Parking Space

Housey Crags

Long Crags

Kelpie Strand

Langleeford

Harthope Burn

Hedgehope Hill

Scald Hill

Langleeford Hope

Harthope Linn

Comb Fell

The Cheviot

Cairn Hill

81

THE WALK

1. "The easiest way to ascend Hedgehope, which is conical and quite different from Cheviot", said W. Ford Robertson, "is to go out as far as Langlee". Nowadays, the preferred route starts ¾ mile further up the Harthope Valley, where the Hawsen Burn joins the Harthope Burn. This is the final point of public vehicular access and there is adequate parking on the large area of grass just prior to the Hawsen Burn **(GR NT953225)** . "In the whole-day walks it will be necessary to carry food with you", advised W. Ford Robertson, so, having checked your sandwiches and high-energy drink, it is time to sling your lightweight, waterproof, hardwearing, superior load-carrying rucksack across your shoulders and to head for the hills. Turn to face up the valley and, on the left hand side of the single track road, a signpost points the way to Housey Crags and your first objective of the walk, Hedgehope Hill.

The start looking towards Housey Crags.

The path alongside the dry stone wall very quickly leads you to a small wooden footbridge over the Harthope Burn and, after a quick climb through the trees, you will see the impressive Housey Crags towering above you. Cross over the step stile and a fairly steep climb up a clear, green path will soon bring you alongside and then behind the crags. Feeling full of beans? Then a quick scramble to the top of the crags will be well rewarded and, whilst these are the best known and most frequently visited of all the Northumberland crags, it is quite possible that you will have them all to yourself.

Housey Crags.

2. Keep with the path, aided by the occasional directional fingerpost, as it ascends onto Long Crags. At more than 420 metres above sea level this airy spot offers a tremendous view towards the shapely Hedgehope Hill and across the valley to The Cheviot and Scald Hill. Once across the crags and over the step stile **(GR NT956213)**, the cotton grass rich moorland of Kelpie Strand makes for pleasant walking. This is very much 'the calm before the storm'.

Hedgehope Hill across Kelpie Strand.

Around the 450 metre contour, the path begins to swing towards the south-west as the climbing begins in earnest. The gradient steepens and the lactic acid begins to bite into your legs. In total, you gain over 260 metres in height in just over half a mile of walking, before finally and quite possibly with some relief, reaching the 714 metre high summit of Hedgehope Hill **(GR NT943197)**. This is certainly the most distinctive of all the Cheviot summits, a place where three fences meet beside a jumble of small stone shelters, a godsend when the wind is battering this exposed spot. The summit is crowned with a triangulation pillar. The views in all directions are outstanding, so take time to complete a full circuit of the top. Having, in the words of W. Ford Robertson, "sat awhile by the side of the cairn and endeavoured to identify as many distant objects as possible", it is time to make tracks.

The Cheviot from Hedgehope Hill.

3. "If, however, you are feeling fit for more", wrote W. Ford Robertson, "you have an excellent opportunity of exploring the peaty ridge of Comb Fell". "It lies", he said, "to the south-west, and may be followed to the head of the Harthope Burn". This is your route ahead. So, with the fence to your left and The Cheviot to your right, begin your easy downhill walk to the lowest point, at 566 metres, along the ridge between Hedgehope Hill and Comb Fell. Here you will need to pick your way through peat hags and across potentially boggy ground. There is no real difficulty, although after prolonged periods of rain the going can be tiresome. Soon the gentle gradient will bring you to the summit of Comb Fell. Although standing at a reasonable 652 metres above sea level and the third highest of the Cheviot Hills, the top is barely noticeable **(GR NT924187)**. There is a difference of only 2 metres in height between the actual summit and the western 'top' of Comb Fell, and these are separated by a distance just short of ½ mile. Continue alongside the post and wire fence across the western top and, after a short and easy descent, you will reach a fence rising up from the Harthope Valley, below you to your right. To the south-west lies the rocky Coldlaw Cairn, one of the most isolated and lonely places in the Cheviot Hills. Do not cross the fence. Turn to your right and, with the fence to the left, begin your descent to the Harthope Valley.

4. The downhill going is relatively straightforward, although you will encounter two substantial peat hags along the way, so be ready to negotiate these by whatever means you find best. You will, in all probability, need to get your hands a tad dirty. Soon you will begin to rise again as you cross the watershed of the Harthope Burn and, when you reach the directional fingerpost **(GR NT906190)**, it is time to go with the flow of the infant burn.

Hedgehope Hill and the watershed of the Harthope Burn.

With the gentle and relaxing sound of trickling water in your ears, cross over to the left hand bank of the burn and head downwards. As you wander along the faint path the burn begins to gain momentum and the rhythm of tumbling water increases. The thin path keeps close to the fledgling burn as it journeys north eastwards between the steep sides of The Cheviot, Comb Fell and Hedgehope Hill, passing along the way, the half-hidden waterfall of Harthope Linn. In his 1926 book W. Ford Robertson wrote, "Soon the lovely surging pool and thundering spout of Harthope Linn will come into view". He indicated that "There is a ledge on the north side upon which you may stand and contemplate the rare

Deep in the Harthope Valley.

beauty of the scene". Here, seemingly cut off from the rest of civilisation, is a truly delightful place to catch your breath and savour the tranquillity before setting out on the last 2½ miles of your walk.

5. Continuing down stream you will, after climbing over a ladder stile, join a farm track which then immediately cuts through a small plantation to the pretty as picture cottage of Langleeford Hope **(GR NT932207)**.

The track to Langleeford Hope.

Once past the building and out into the open, the views down the valley broaden, with Long Crags and Housey Crags slipping effortlessly into the picture. Before long you will catch sight of the white-washed walls of Langleeford peeping out of the trees on the opposite side of the burn. This farm was mentioned as long ago as 1552 and is, perhaps, most famous as the holiday retreat of one of Scotland`s best known writers. In `Walks from Wooler`, W. Ford Robertson referred to the farm as "the house at which Sir Walter Scott stayed in 1791", by all accounts a happy holiday for the young writer who enjoyed the fishing, walking and the sight of the pretty dairy-maid who brought him goat`s whey to drink every morning. The tarmac valley road is rapidly re-joined and all too quickly you will be back beside the Hawsen Burn, contented in the knowledge that you have completed two of the four highest climbs which were considered by W. Ford Robertson to be, "within reach of Wooler". Perhaps, like him, you will feel that "Few who are in process of ascending them will wish any of these hills were higher". On the other hand with energy to burn, maybe not!

FGS Grading

Grading is F9 [D1, N2, T2, R2, H2]

Distance	1	6 – 12 miles
Navigation	2	Competent navigation skills needed
Terrain	2	25 -50% on graded track or path 50 – 75% off / single track
Remoteness	2	Countryside not in close proximity to habitation – less than 20% of the route within 2 miles
Height	2	Over 125 ft per mile

**Beside the bridleway to the Harthope Valley.
Walk 8 The Lambden Valley Hills.**

WALK 8: THE LAMBDEN VALLEY HILLS

The Lambden Valley lies in the shadow of The Cheviot with no public vehicular right of access. As a consequence, the valley slumbers in peaceful isolation. "The whole glen is beautiful", wrote W. Ford Robertson and so it is. On the northern side of the valley rise three often-ignored hills, Coldburn, Preston, and Broadhope and, when linked together in a single walk, these hills offer intimate views of the `dark` side of The Cheviot. This is a `warts and all` portrait of the north `face` of Northumberland`s most iconic hill. It is a walk of contrasts.

DISTANCE: 7.5 miles (12.1 km)
ASCENT: 2083 feet (635 metres)
TERRAIN: Mainly clear tracks, paths and traces, in places rough, and one short stretch of tarmac.
TIME: 4 hours
START: Hawsen Burn, Harthope Valley (GR NT954225)

Grid References

Hawsen Burn	954 225
Fence	934 229
Ford	913 234
Metal gate	908 241
Coldburn Hill	902 241
Preston Hill	922 238
Broadhope Hill	932 234
Stile	944 233
Hawsen Burn	954 225

FGS Grading

Grading is F10 [D1, N2, T2, R2, H3]

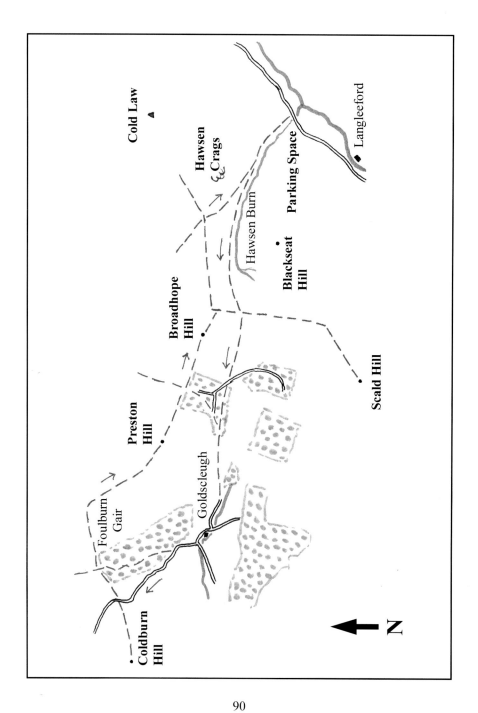

THE WALK

1. "The road is not very suitable for a motor car", wrote W. Ford Robertson when describing the route through the Harthope Valley. He suggested that, "You may lessen the fatigue of the outing by having a horse conveyance", to a point nearer to your main objective. The narrow, sinuous road through the beautiful hill-lined valley is now perfectly suitable for cars so, with little need to saddle-up your horse, you can concentrate on making your way from the morning streets of Wooler to the point where the Hawsen Burn slips downhill to greet the delightful Harthope Burn. There is ample parking nearby **(GR NT954225)**. Time now to fasten up your gaiters, check your stylish, stainless steel vacuum flask, pull on your warm, ear-hugging hat and to make tracks for the circular stone sheep stell on the north side of the valley road, adjacent to the Hawsen Burn. Keeping to the right hand side of the burn, climb straight up the facing slope to pick up a clear path heading up the narrow valley. After a short distance you will join a rough stone track and, within a further 200 metres, you will reach a directional fingerpost on your left. Leave the track and follow the thin public footpath which, in due course, passes another circular stone sheep stell. Keep with the thin path, avoiding the temptation to rejoin the track which, for a short distance only, runs immediately above you. Behind you, the impressive and ever-popular Housey Crags are slowly disappearing into the distance.

2. The adder is the only poisonous snake native to Britain and it is not unusual

Housey Crags from the Hawsen Burn.

to encounter one in the Cheviot Hills. "Always to be killed at sight", was the advice given by W. Ford Robertson, a course of action now totally outdated. The adder is protected under the Wildlife and Countryside Act 1981 and it is an offence to either kill or injure them in any way. They are not naturally aggressive and are best left well alone. As the gradient begins to ease, the burn is left behind and the thin path leads you across the heather covered col between Broadhope and Scald Hills. Two directional fingerposts will keep you on the `straight and narrow`, leading you to a post and wire fence running from north to south **(GR NT934229)**. You are now looking down into the head of the lonely Lambden Valley with the mass of The Cheviot to the left and the rounded tops of Broadhope and Preston Hills to your immediate right. You now need to turn right for some 200 metres as far as the small step stile. Cross over and continue on a downhill trajectory, on a clear path, in the direction of an old forestry track. Once reached, turn right towards a small plantation and, in turn, cross over the feeble remains of a step stile lying next to a five bar gate. Still with the track, follow the yellow public footpath directional arrows into the plantation and pass through the trees on a thin wavering path. Once out into daylight, head diagonally down the lower slopes of Preston Hill and, keeping on a westwards course, the yellow directional arrows will lead you, via a shallow ford, across the Lambden Burn.

Crossing the Lambden Burn.

On reaching the opposite bank, go over the step stile which is close to the trees beside the burn. Soon you will come to the Goldscleugh Burn, step over, turn left and, after going through two five bar gates, pass behind the farm buildings and head across the field towards a gate and the adjoining public footpath signpost.

3. The white-walled farmstead of Goldscleugh is one of only three properties in the valley and the only one which is still occupied as a permanent dwelling. This was described by W. Ford Robertson as "a shepherd's cottage". Once through the gate, turn right along the tarmac road towards the farmstead and, after some 100 metres, leave the road to your left and cross the Lambden Burn via a slightly-higher than ankle deep ford **(GR NT913234)**. To your right, climbing across the western slopes of Preston Hill, there is a plantation and you will now wind your way uphill on a good, green track with the edge of the trees always close at hand. You are following, initially at least, "the path that leads up the eastern shoulder of Coldburn Hill", as described by W. Ford Robertson in his 1926 book. When the public footpath disappears into the plantation, do not follow this as your route stays with the green track as far as an old metal gate **(GR NT908241)**. As you climb towards the gate do take the time to give a backwards glance as there are superb views of the valley and the picture postcard Goldscleugh. Pass through the gate and, with the summit of Coldburn Hill lying due

Goldscleugh from the slopes of Coldburn Hill.

west, head towards a row of 12 small wooden shooting butts which climb towards the top of the hill. Aim for the sixth butt from the right along a track which has been cut through the heather. When this is reached, turn left in front

The twin-cairned Coldburn Hill.

of the butts and climb to the twin-cairned summit **(GR NT902241)**.

4. At 485 metres above a distant sea level, Coldburn Hill enjoys splendid views towards the College Valley, the Schil and the impressive rocky cleft to the south. This is where the Bizzle Burn flows from its source, high on the summit plateau of Northumberland's premier mountain, down to the Lambden Burn. In his book, W. Ford Robertson seemed slightly lukewarm, describing "The Bizzle" as, "the gloomy chasm on the north face of Cheviot". However, he was much more enthusiastic about picnics, saying, "When the time arrives for the mid-day halt and lunch, you will know, as you may have never done before, how good a sandwich can taste and how cool and refreshing is water from a mountain stream". You have now arrived at the most pleasant of picnic spots, so

The cairn on Preston Hill.

lay your waterproof on the ground and have a good tuck in. Now return back to the metal gate and, instead of passing through and returning to the valley, turn to your left and follow the fence past the north-western edge of the plantation and then above Foulburn Gair. The word 'Gair' has Anglo-Saxon origins and simply means 'a pointed piece of land where streams meet'. As you reach higher ground the fence turns towards the south-east and, as you climb towards the 526 metre high summit of Preston Hill **(GR NT922238)**, you will pass a large cairn standing next to the fence. With miles of empty moorland, except for the isolated farmstead of Commonburn House, stretching away to your left and the cold north face of The Cheviot staring down at you to your right, this is a truly lonely place. It is also the highest point of your walk.

The slopes of Preston Hill.

5. Continue across the summit, with the post and wire fence to your right, before descending sharply down a thin rocky path. On reaching flatter ground you will have dropped some 100 metres in height in just 500 metres of walking and are standing on what was described by W. Ford Robertson as, "The swyre between Broadhope and Preston Hill". During the days of the Border troubles this swyre, or pass, was regularly used by Scottish raiders. To your left rises the Broadstruthers Burn, whilst to your right lies the remnants of a recently harvested plantation, the head of the Lambden Valley and your outward route. Continue across the swyre, take a deep breath and begin your steep climb up the slopes of Broadhope Hill, regaining as you go, virtually all of the 100 metres in height you lost little more than a handful of minutes ago. The summit **(GR NT932234)**, which is marked by the most miniscule of cairns, lies slightly to

Boundary stone on Broadhope Hill.

your left and stands at a height of 517 metres. Still keeping close to the fence you will quickly pass an old boundary stone carved with the letter `H` on one side and `S` on the other. The views begin to stretch out ahead, with the crags of the Harthope Valley, Langlee, Middleton, Housey and Long, and the long back of Cold Law all unmistakeable. At the first fence junction turn sharp left and,

Descending Broadhope Hill.

when the fence again turns 90°, follow it to the right. Now begins the rapid descent down the eastern side of Broadhope Hill culminating at the bridleway running between Broadstruther, away to your left, and the Harthope Valley, to your right. Cross over the step stile **(GR NT944233)** and, as your boots touch the firm gravel track, you will spot, just to your right, another initial-carved boundary stone.

Now it is an easy walk downhill on the track heading, initially, towards the Hawsen Burn and then above it. Be careful, when this track cuts across the burn close to Butterwell Sike, to take the thin path which stays with the left bank and along which you began the day`s walk. All too soon this will deliver you back to the Harthope Valley and the near perfect circular stone sheep stell. As you sit next to your car, your empty boots lying on the sheep-cropped grass, maybe you will feel, as did W. Ford Robertson all those years ago, that the Cheviot Hills are indeed, "a paradise for the pedestrian".

FGS Grading

Grading is F10 [D1, N2, T2, R2, H3]

Distance	1	6 – 12 miles
Navigation	2	Competent navigation skills needed
Terrain	2	25 -50% on graded track or path 50 – 75% off / single track
Remoteness	2	Countryside not in close proximity to habitation – less than 20% of the route within 2 miles
Height	3	Over 250 ft per mile

POSTSCRIPT

The windswept summit cairns, the quiet hidden cleughs, the purple heather moors, the bracken-covered hillsides, the rain-filled peat pools, the February snowfields, the Spring gorse, the busy burns, the billowing clouds in a wide Cheviot sky, the solitude. In the big picture, little has changed since W. Ford Robertson wrote his 1926-published book, 'Walks from Wooler'.

It is, as they say, all in the detail. Roads have become accessible to the motor car, better access has brought a greater number of walkers to the hills, waymarkers have been erected, popular footpaths have become eroded, triangulation pillars have appeared and have subsequently become redundant, afforestation has altered the face of many hillsides, farm cottages have become holiday homes, shepherds have become quad bike riders, shooting butts have been built and distance-shrinking Land Rover tracks have been constructed. Some for the better, others not.

In his book, W. Ford Robertson wrote, "If you are in walking trim......an outing among these solitudes.....is a happy experience that can never be forgotten". And so it remains. The air is still as fresh, the rain is still as wet, the wind is still as cold and the views are still as lovely. Eighty years or so have done nothing to diminish that.

A waymarker and a big Cheviot view.

APPENDIX

Ferguson Grading System (`FGS`)

1. Introduction
The FGS has been adopted as a means of assessing the nature and severity of the various walks in this book and the abilities and equipment needed to tackle each one safely. The FGS was developed by Stuart Ferguson, a long time fell and trail runner, climber, mountaineer, mountain-biker and general outdoor enthusiast. In the opinion of Trailguides the FGS is the most accurate and comprehensive grading system for comparing off-road walking, running and mountain-biking routes anywhere in the country.

2. The System
Tables 1 & 2, set out below, are used in order to give a grading to each route. Table 1 sets out three categories of country that a route could potentially cross, together with a range of factors that would need to be considered when tackling that route. The three categories are, Trail, Fell and Mountain, and after assessing which category best fits the route, a letter, either `T`, `F` or `M`, is allocated to that route. Where a route does not fit perfectly into one of the three categories the closest category is allocated.

Table 2 deals with five specific aspects of the route, distance, navigation, terrain, remoteness and height gain, and each one is allocated a letter, `D`, `N`, `T`, `R`, and `H`. Each letter is also given a severity score from the range 0-3 or 0-4, in respect of distance (`D`). The higher the number, the more severe the route. The five severity scores are then added together to give an overall score. The overall score is then put with the Table 1 category letter (i.e. `T`, `F` or `M`).

In order to show how the grading has been determined for each walk in this book, the five individual severity scores are set out, in square brackets, immediately after the actual grading. So, for example, Walk 3 The Road to Tom Tallon's Crag has a grading of F9 [D1, N2, T2, R2, H2], indicating that it is a Fell Category walk with a total severity score of 9. This is made up of the five specific severity scores, for distance (`D`), navigation (`N`), terrain (`T`), remoteness (`R`) and height gain (`H`), of 1, 2, 2, 2 and 2 respectively. The highest total severity score which can be achieved is 16 and the lowest total severity score achievable is 0.

The table which accompanies the grading at the end of each walk sets out the specific factors, extracted from Table 2, that need to be considered when tackling that particular walk.

TABLE 1

	TRAIL	FELL	MOUNTAIN
Description	Lowland and forest areas including urban, cultivated and forested locations.	Moorlands and upland areas which may include some upland cultivated and forestry areas plus possibly remote locations.	Upland and mountain areas including remote and isolated locations.
Height	Not usually above 1,000 feet but may go up to 2,500 feet	Usually above 1,000 feet, up to 2,500 feet and above.	Usually above 2,500 feet and up to 4,000 feet.
Way-marking	Usually	Limited	None
Terrain	Usually graded paths, tracks and trails but may include some off-trail	May include some graded paths, tracks and trails but mainly off-trail	Virtually all off-trail
Height gain	Limited height gain	May include considerable height gain	May include some severe height gain.
Effects of weather	Very limited effect	May be prone to sudden weather changes	Extreme weather a possibility
Navigational skills	None to basic	Basic to competent	Competent to expert
Equipment	Walking shoes/boots. Possibly waterproofs Food and drink dependant upon route.	3/4 season walking boots. Full waterproof cover. Possibly map and compass dependant upon route. Food and drink dependant upon route.	Mountain boots. Full waterproof cover. Map and compass. Food and drink
Escape Routes	Yes	Some	Some to nil

TABLE 2

Score	0	1	2	3	4
Distance	Up to 6 miles	6 – 12 miles	12 – 18 miles	18 miles +	24 miles +
Navigation	No navigation skills needed	Basic navigation skills needed	Competent navigation skills needed	Expert navigation skills needed	
Terrain	75% + on graded track or path	50 – 75% on graded track or path 25 – 50% off track	25 -50% on graded track or path 50 – 75% off track	Under 25% on graded track or path Over 75% off track	
Remoteness	Urban	Countryside in fairly close proximity to habitation – at least 80% of the route within 2 miles	Countryside not in close proximity to habitation – less than 20% of the route within 2 miles	Remote, isolated location	
Height gain	Less than 100 ft per mile	Over 100 ft per mile	Over 125 ft per mile	Over 250 ft per mile	

Notes to Table 2

Graded paths = Well established paths with a stable surface.

Escape routes = The opportunity to cut the route short and return to the start without completing the full course in the event of weather changes or unforeseen incidents.

The Author

Geoff Holland

Geoff is a Northumbrian by birth and for the past thirty seven years has lived in Monkseaton, a hop, skip and jump from the North Sea coast. For most of his years he has enjoyed the outdoors as a hill walker, fell runner and mountain-biker. In particular he has developed a love for the hills of his home county, the Cheviots.

Over the years Geoff has written extensively about the Cheviot Hills and his work, including photographs, has appeared in magazines such as `Country Walking`, `TGO (The Great Outdoors)` and `The Northumbrian`. He is the author of four popular walking guidebooks including `The Cheviot Hills`, 'The Hills of Upper Coquetdale', 'Walks on the Wild Side: The Cheviot Hills' and 'Walks from Wooler' published by Trailguides. A number of his poems have appeared in books, magazines, journals and online.

Geoff's passion for the Cheviots has lead him to set-up and operate an acclaimed website dedicated to walking in the Cheviot Hills and this is now recognised as being one of the best walking websites in the North of England. He is married with a grown up daughter and son. He also has two young granddaughters.

The author (and bike) on the summit of Windy Gyle.

Walking North East

Walking North East is the brand name for the walking publications produced by Trailguides and reflects the pride that we, as North Easterners, have in our countryside, our history and our culture.

Based in Darlington, we are a small independent publisher specialising in guide-books centred on the North Eastern counties of England. Our target is to produce guides that are as user-friendly, easy to use and provide as much information as possible and all in an easily readable format. In essence to increase the enjoyment of the user and to showcase the very best of the great North Eastern countryside. Our series of books explores the heritage of us all and lets you see your region with new eyes, these books are written to not just take you on a walk but to investigate, explore and understand the objects, places and history that has shaped not just the countryside but also the people of this corner of England.

If you've enjoyed following the routes in this guide and want news and details of other publications that are being developed under the Walking North East label then look at the company website at **www.trailguides.co.uk**

Comments and, yes, criticisms, are always welcomed especially if you discover a change to a route. Contact us by email through the website or by post at Trail-guides Limited, 35 Carmel Road South, Darlington, Co Durham DL3 8DQ.

Other walking books from Walking North East.
At the time of publication the following books are also available but with new titles being regularly added to our publication list keep checking our website.

Northumberland.
The Cheviot Hills.
Walks from Wooler.
The Hills of Upper Coquetdale.
Walks from Kirknewton
Walks Around Rothbury and Coquetdale
Walks on the Wild Side: The Cheviot Hills

County Durham.
Hamsterley Forest.
The Barningham Trail.
Ancient Stones.
The High Hills of Teesdale.
Walks from Stanhope.

North Yorkshire.
The Hills of Upper Swaledale.
Walks from Gunnerside
Walks around Reeth and Upper Swaledale

Walking North East.
Visit our website and sign up to receive our free newsletter, Walking North East, dedicated to walking in North Eastern England. Full of news, views and articles relating to this the forgotten corner of England.

Acknowledgements
are due to the late W. Ford Robertson, whose `Walks from Wooler` was the inspiration for this book, to 'The Northumbrian' magazine who set the ball rolling by publishing my article `In the Footsteps of W. Ford Robertson`, to Tom Johnston of the Glendale Trust and John Martin the YHA (England & Wales) Volunteer Archivist & Historian for providing so much fascinating information about the Wooler Youth Hostel, to Stu Ferguson for the use of his excellent grading system and to my wife Ellie for her unwavering support

---

Emerging into daylight off Kenterdale Hill.
Walk 4. The Hart Heugh Glidders

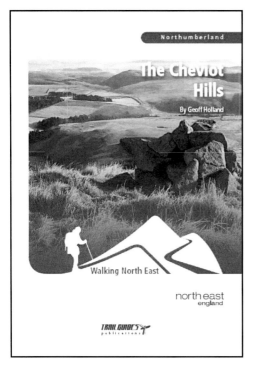

The Cheviot Hills

Geoff Holland

The Cheviot Hills stand on the northern edge of England at the heart of the Northumberland National Park. They roll across the border into Scotland like a tide of small, green waves. These are wild and expansive hills where the echo of history can be heard from every windswept hill and in every tranquil valley. This is ideal walking country.

On each of the eight self-guided walks the reader will uncover a small piece of the Cheviot jigsaw. They will follow less than ordinary routes to summit cairns and distant views. Along the way they will encounter cleughs, burns, sikes, crags, shins, dodds, hopes, linns, shanks and a whole lot more. This is an appetite whetting selection of walks in the Cheviot Hills.

The Hills of Upper Coquetdale

Geoff Holland

The River Coquet rises on the remote upper slopes of Brownhart Law, close to the Roman military complex of Chew Green, and for the first 10 miles of a long and wayward journey to the North Sea this magnificent river rubs shoulders with some of the finest hills in Northumberland. Here, seemingly light years from the stresses and strains of 21st century life, the `Hills of Upper Coquetdale` offer walking of the highest quality.

Written by the author of two previous books of walks, `The Cheviot Hills` and `Walks from Wooler`, this latest book contains eight totally new self-guided walks with detailed, easy to follow route descriptions and a rucksack full of fascinating information about the area. This is a unique collection of walks in the most tranquil corner of England.

Informative, interesting and entertaining, guide books don't really come any better than this" North East Lifestyle magazine

This is fabulous walking country, in the company of one of the UK's most respected guide writers" Country Walking magazine

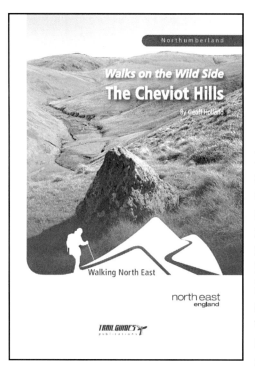

Walks on the Wild Side: The Cheviot Hills

Geoff Holland

In the great scheme of matters mountainous the Cheviot Hills are not especially big hills, rising to a mere 815 metres (2674 feet) at their highest point. However, these are lonely hills of sweeping vistas and far-off horizons, where wild goats roam and the call of the curlew echoes across centuries of a violent and bloody past. These are predominantly grass-covered hills of long, shapely ridges and deep hidden valleys. These are hills which offer walking of the finest quality.

Written by the author of three popular books of walks, `The Cheviot Hills`, `Walks from Wooler` and `The Hills of Upper Coquetdale`, this latest book contains eight totally unique self-guided walks with detailed, simple to follow route descriptions and a sandwich box full of easily digestible information. These are walks designed to tempt inquisitive and adventurous walkers outside their normal walking boundaries. These are walks for the connoisseur with a taste for something just that little bit different. So pull on your boots and take `a walk on the wild side`.